WHEN WILL WE LAUGH AGAIN?
Living and Dealing with Anorexia Nervosa and Bulimia

WHEN WILL WE LAUGH AGAIN?

Living and Dealing with Anorexia Nervosa and Bulimia

Edited and written by Barbara P. Kinoy *in collaboration with* Estelle B. Miller, John A. Atchley *and the* Book Committee of the American Anorexia/Bulimia Association

Columbia University Press
New York 1984

Frontispiece: Creative embroidery by Patricia Gal DePol.

Library of Congress Cataloging in Publication Data

Kinoy, Barbara P.
When will we laugh again?

Bibliography: p.
Includes index.
1. Anorexia nervosa. 2. Bulimarexia. I. Title.
[DNLM: 1. Anorexia nervosa. 2. Appetite disorders.
WM 175 W567]
RC552.A5K56 1984 616.85'2 83-26230
ISBN 0-231-05638-9 (alk. paper)

Columbia University Press
New York Guildford, Surrey

Printed in the United States of America

Clothbound editions of Columbia University Press Books are Smyth-sewn and printed on permanent and durable acid-free paper

Design: K. Venezio

This book is
dedicated to all
our children that
they may realize
their worth
beyond
appearance
and that
they may enjoy
the sensations
of life
without
fear.

Contents

Contributors

John A. Atchley, M.D., president, American Anorexia/Bulimia Association; assistant clinical professor of psychiatry, College of Physicians and Surgeons, Columbia University; staff member of the New York State Psychiatric Institute and Columbia Presbyterian Medical Center; and in private practice.

Arthur H. Crisp, M.D., D.Sc., FRCP, FRCP(E), FRC Psych., head of Department of Psychiatry, St. George's Hospital Medical School, University of London; author of numerous articles, and of *Anorexia Nervosa: Let Me Be.*

Sheila Freed, M.S., M.T. (A.S.C.P.), American Anorexia/Bulimia Association Book Committee member, AA/BA Special Committee on Insurance Problems; Research in Medical Biology.

Adele Holman, D.S.W., American Anorexia/Bulimia Association Book Committee member, professional co-leader AA/BA Self-Help Groups; author of *Family Assessment: An Approach to Child Neglect and Abuse*, and *Family Assessment: Tools for Understanding and Intervention*; adjunct associate professor, Adelphi University; psychotherapist in private practice; Director of Clinical Projects, Family Institute of Westchester.

Susan Heeger, free-lance writer.

Barbara P. Kinoy, ACSW, Ph.D., American Anorexia/Bulimia Association Board member, Book Committee member, professional co-leader of AA/BA Self-Help Groups; staff member, Wilkins Center for Eating Disorders; and psychoanalyst in private practice.

Estelle B. Miller, M.S.W., founder and executive director of the American Anorexia/Bulimia Association, Book Committee member, professional co-leader of AA/BA Self-Help groups; and psychotherapist in private practice; currently a doctoral candidate.

Lynn MacGregor, American Anorexia/Bulimia Association Book Committee member, founding Board member of AA/BA.

Foreword

Arthur H. Crisp

I first came into contact with what is now called the American Anorexia/Bulimia Association several years ago, and was rapidly impressed by its professional maturity and openness. It has been a pleasure for me to maintain this contact and I am especially pleased to be invited to write a brief introduction to this book.

The origins of anorexia nervosa lie partly in our society and are a political and cultural indictment of it. In this book the anorectics and their families speak to us and leave us with that subtle notion that, while every human problem is unique, sympathy and understanding of a kind that can be helpful can arise within a family or caring group. Furthermore, that caring is not only to be delegated to professional and perhaps narrow specialists but craves expression and can be harnessed for the general good from among those afflicted with or touched by the condition. The idea of harnessing complementary strengths for the common good within a broadly based self-help organization, and of taking advantage of that very human quality of seeing others' problems more clearly than our own has been brought to a fine pitch in the American Anorexia/Bulimia Association.

Anorexia nervosa is a cruel disorder arising as a desperate attempt by the individual concerned to cope with life but which leaves her physically and socially crippled. This book allows this whole perspective and also recognizes the potential for growth in sufferers. It conveys a credible message of hope to everyone. The message is that the task may well be possible—it will be daunting but there are those who want to help and can often do so. I think that you may discover that this is so through reading this book.

Acknowledgments

We wish to acknowledge and thank the families, sufferers, and the many others who wrote lengthy letters to inform us of their particular experience. Their copious, rich, and varied accounts have given us information for a composite picture of families and individuals who have lived through, or who are now living through, this crisis. It is from their generosity and courage that we have been able to develop an understanding of the attitudes and feelings involved in the family's experience of anorexia nervosa and bulimia.

The following people participated in the taped sessions and telephone tapings and contributed in other ways.

Cynthia Barber
Hathi Blackman
Mavis Clinedinst
Carolyn V. Collis
Clyde H. Estes
Elizabeth K. Estes
Sheila Fallik
Diane A. Fink
Tom Foley
Sheila Freed
Lillian Gould
Claire Guten
Susan Heeger
Adele Holman
Donna Jabbour
Joan V. A. Johnson
Barbara P. Kinoy
Cami Klein
Doris Knoeller
Nancy Kramer
Retta Lane
Thomas A. Lane
Joan Lipton
Theodore Lipton
Judy Ludvik
Lynn MacGregor
John C. MacGregor
Nicki Meyer
David Miller
Estelle B. Miller
Malaine Miller
Mitchell Miller

Paul Nussbaum
Stevie Nussbaum
Patricia De Pol
John De Pol
Barbara Remmers
Hilda Remmers
Carol Scheinholtz
Richard Scheinholtz
Judy Spindel
Alynnore Tom
Kathy Welkens
Roberta Wolff
Rita Zwirn
Stacey Zwirn

Many others participated but did not wish to be acknowledged.

Theirs is a profound contribution of their own thoughts and feelings, given in the spirit of illuminating the ordeal for others with understanding that was gleaned only by living through the crisis and with feelings that only one who had experienced the daily details, as part of the family or as the sufferer, could know. Their true reward will perhaps be found only through others who learn to survive and overcome this catastrophe of anorexia/bulimia.

Our efforts could not have been sustained without the assistance of the Nametre Company which gave us funds. Moreover, with this gift we were given the trust that we could coordinate the valuable material that families had to offer. The AABA Board extended that trust by providing extra money to complete the work. As we proceeded, we were encouraged further by a grant from Mr. and Mrs. Herbert Smith, who suffered the tragic loss of their daughter through this illness. We thank them for their faith in our efforts.

We wish to acknowledge the assistance of John Gibson, A.C.S.W., who collated our questionnaires, extracting cogent material that could point up certain issues and help us expand upon some others that emerged in taped sessions.

Our taped sessions were carefully prepared, almost unobtrusive in the technical aspects of taping, so that participants felt fairly unencumbered and unselfconscious during the actual taping. We acknowledge and thank sound technician Daniel P. Kinoy.

Our procedures were immensely eased and smoothed by the careful assistance of Janice Garvey, Linda Rothenberg, M.A., and Marion Donahue. Janice Garvey ably kept the various pieces of the manuscript going as it was being pulled together. We thank each for their special assistance.

Last, we wish to acknowledge each other in our various tasks in the cooperative effort undertaken in putting this book together. We have had different roles, and often different views, although our agreements have been far greater. Our investments are deep in the fabric of this material. We ache for ourselves and for those others who must survive this ordeal. We want it to be no mere survival, but one that enables and enriches the capacity to live, work, relate, to endure anxiety and to appreciate joy and laughter.

The American Anorexia/Bulimia Association, Inc.
President: John A. Atchley
Executive Director: Estelle B. Miller
Book Committee: Sheila Freed
Adele Holman
Lynn MacGregor
Estelle B. Miller
Barbara P. Kinoy, Editor

Introduction: It Takes a Combination of Many Things

Estelle B. Miller

At a recent meeting of the association a parent of an anorexic asked me about my daughter who is a recovering anorexic. With a gigantic smile on my face, I informed her that my daughter had telephoned me the day after we had attended her college graduation to say that she had menstruated for the first time in her life. I said that it must be symbolic, my daughter is ready to grow up.

The woman burst into tears. I became all choked up myself and apologized for upsetting her. With great urgency she asked, "What was the one thing that's making her better?" I replied, "It's never one thing, but always a combination of life situations and events that lead to recovery." I also felt it was the love, support, and guidance from our family and close friends over a period of years that had definitely sustained her. My husband and I had undergone psychotherapy before our daughter developed anorexia nervosa. I had then continued in therapy over a very long period of time to learn how to cope with my own frustrations with this life-threatening illness.

You will ask, as I do, is my daughter fully recovered? Now

twenty-one, she says that her recovery began when she was twenty years old, after she had been anorexic for five years.

It usually takes another five years for normal weight to stabilize and for the menstrual period to become normal. It generally takes many years for the individual to develop new constructive habits in dealing with life situations, without resorting to obsessing about food, diet, and weight.

Thinking back now, I realize that her anorexia started several months before she was fifteen years old, in April of 1976. Around that time I had attended a mental health conference where I had seen a video tape of an anorexic's progress during family therapy. The tape and lecture were informative, but also very startling. I had thought that it was such a terrible waste for a young person to starve herself so deliberately. Only a week later I became aware, when she took off her heavy winter clothes, that my own daughter was doing just that. She had been dieting and losing weight for three months without anyone noticing. It had apparently started in January 1976 when I told her that her father thought she needed to lose a couple of pounds. I had no idea what a loaded remark that was, because she then took it to an extreme. I had not realized that someone with this predisposition is so overly sensitive.

I was shocked. I suspected that it was anorexia. I thought that with all the psychotherapy we had had it couldn't happen in our family. We were such seemingly aware people. Thus I began taking her to doctors: an internist, a psychiatrist, and a gynecologist. At the same time I was hoping that it was a temporary condition that would go away by itself. She had always been such a *sensible* child. I also kept denying that it could be this serious condition. I hoped that we, her parents and doctors, could appeal to her good sense. Nothing worked. At that time she weighed eighty pounds, and then she lost three more pounds. After eight months, we had to hospitalize her under the expert care of a pediatrician and a female psychiatrist.

The worst moment for me came when I visited her in the hospital right after the doctors had given the order to force feed her. I discovered her lying in her bed with a tube in her nose and her eyes puffy from crying. I was in tears myself—enraged because of the anguish she was putting me through, but at the same time upset that she was being treated like an animal who had no ability to reason. I believed then and still do that we had no choice but to agree to her treatment. I would hospitalize her again if I thought it were a life-and-death situation.

She had entered the hospital on December 2, 1976, when she was fifteen and one-half years old. She remained there for one month. She had reached eighty-eight pounds when she was released but lost four pounds shortly thereafter. She continued with medical and psychiatric care as an outpatient for two and a half more years on a weekly basis. She chose not to continue therapy when she went away to college, even though she was still very thin. We did not agree with her decision to stop therapy, but since she was of legal age, we were powerless to insist. As she gained weight through the next three years, she grew two and one quarter inches. Also, her attitude improved for the better. She opened up much more and her relationship with me and with others became more loving.

In our examination of our household, we recognized some factors that may have contributed to her condition. We were overly concerned about being thin; we followed "excellent" health habits. She evidently took all this to an extreme. We were, and are, usually openly expressive and affectionate. She, however, was less so. I used to compliment her about being so cool and calm, without realizing that I might be encouraging her to be stoic and to hold back expressions and feelings. She was the one out of my three children (she is the middle child) whom the pediatrician saw less often because whe was so healthy. She had had all the childhood diseases and practically no other illnesses.

Many theoreticians say that anorexia nervosa occurs when the child is over-protected and when the family members are excessively involved with one another. At the time, in our family, this did not seem the case. She may have had *too* much freedom in her early years. However, I feel that she is a product of her home life, among many other factors. I reflect about her early life and my life then. When she was an infant, she was very attached to me. When she was two years old, I gave birth to my third child, after which I suffered a post partum depression lasting for several months. She never seemed to be aware of changes or show any disappointment.

As she grew, she became a compliant, good girl in her adolescence. She saw a mother trying to manage a household and career, and she sensed the conflicts I was having. I feel that she incorporated them into herself. She wanted very much to help me and make things easier for me. She cooked meals and even typed my papers. I allowed her to be burdened with responsibilities. She became too serious for such a young person. People would say later on she was sixteen going on thirty.

I hope that someday she will write about her experiences and feelings and give us some insight into the cause of her anorexia. In the meantime I can only speculate.

As a child I had come from a single parent family. We were on the welfare rolls for many years during the Depression. I had graduated from a tuition-free college and met my husband there. All my life I had tried to overcome adversities and my life's goal was to assist others to do the same. Yet I felt helpless because I couldn't help my own daughter to get well. Her doctors advised me to keep away from the symptoms of diet, food, and her weight and just allow the power struggles between us to surface.

After a year and a half of living with this on a daily basis—the doubts, the fears, the anger, the guilt, the resentment—I realized that I was doing everything possible to help her. I had often tried to find solace in prayer during those dark days. Now it was up to her to decide that she wanted to get better. I kept looking for some good to come out of it all, but I found no answers. So I decided to create and develop a way to help parents cope as I was trying to do. It was at that time that I decided to start this organization.

Awhile ago I visited one of our affiliate chapters in Atlanta as a consultant. I was asked to lead the parents' self-help group with two parents. I told the other parent leaders before the meeting that I was there in the group as a professional to elicit questions but that the group members should turn to each other for alternate solutions.

At the meeting the parent leader introduced me as the founder of the association, the visiting resource person, and an expert in the field. Since I don't believe that there are experts in this field and am leery of any who say that they are (and also those who quote statistics), I was made uncomfortable by the parent's comments. Before I could respond another parent in the group asked if I were a recovered anorexic or a parent of one. She had had enough rhetoric, she said, from experts.

I told her that I was a parent and recounted my experiences with the illness. My comments to them were provocative. It brought me down off my professional pedestal to their experiential level. I realized that they related to me as a human being who had also suffered much.

In the beginning my intention was to start a parent support program on a local and national level. I discussed this idea with my daughter and the others in the family who would be affected. Her doctor felt that in order to protect her from being exposed or possibly mocked and looked at with morbid fascination, I would have to face everyone as a mental health professional interested in a new cause, that is, not as a parent of an anorexic. My daughter also needed space during her adolescence to learn how to adapt and develop her own new ideas. Sometimes this decision has been difficult, because people would question my motivation and would become suspicious that I was doing this to further my own interests. During this time I received my master's degree in psychiatric social work from Yeshiva University. I appealed to a community organization faculty member at the university to assist me with constructive ideas in starting a new organization. In addition, I was encouraged and assisted by a deeply concerned colleague, Dr. Noel C. Galen, a psychiatrist, who became the association's first president.

On January 11, 1978, after two and a half months of careful preparation, the first board meeting of the Anorexia Nervosa Aid

Society, Inc., took place. (The name has been changed twice since then.) Twenty-five persons attended. They were anorexics, parents, psychiatrists, teachers, journalists, school nurses, internists, pediatricians, lawyers, social workers, and concerned citizens of the community. The purpose was to make the society broad-based and varied. The parents and anorexics were the persons who assisted with the various tasks, which provided them with a rewarding outlet as it did for me. We listened to each other and most decisions were unanimous—from the name, to its purposes, to its programs, and to its goals. The name was changed a year and a half later by our president, Dr. John A. Atchley, to reflect the fact of going "national" and developing chapters. Our programs have been expanded as our needs have grown.

The definition of anorexia nervosa, "a serious illness of deliberate self-starvation with profound psychiatric and physical components," was decided upon at the charter board meeting, as was also our purpose—"to provide services and programs for anyone involved with AN and to aid in the education, research, cure, and prevention of this illness." Recently, however, we have added, after AN, "and other eating disorders" and the definition of bulimia, because the bulimia syndrome has been increasing. Our name now, American Anorexia/Bulimia Association, reflects this change. We have been contacted by mail or telephone by many who were anorexic in their teens and then became bulimic.

The latest "Diagnostic and Statistical Manual-III" (DSM III) of the American Psychiatric Association separates the two disorders into two areas, but we differ because the two have so much in common, and a person may fluctuate from anorexia to bulimia in the course of the illness. In each there is the fear of becoming fat and preoccupation with food, diet, and weight.

At our first board meeting several anorexics were present who expressed a need for their own support group. There were already about thirty young people who had contacted us because of recent publicity. We decided to meet once a week in my office, stipulating that medical and psychiatric care was mandatory for the participants. The parents group started several weeks later in the town hall near my office.

I remember vividly that first anorexic self-help meeting held in my office in late January 1978, ten days after our charter board meeting. There were fifteen persons, all anorexics except for Patricia DePol, a recovered anorexic who functioned as a professional group leader, and myself. I remember my anxiety and fears—what would we talk about?—and my personal and emotional reaction at seeing so many young people with the same affliction. It turned out to be exciting and emotionally draining, just as all the meetings have been since.

I found myself caught up in what they were saying and reaching a new level of understanding of the illness. I felt compassion and empathy in a way I never could before that day. I felt chills as I listened to their pain and I tried to help them in a non-directive and supportive way.

During our first year, while our general meetings, held five times a year with guest lecturers and communication workshops, were drawing hundreds of families and professionals, the anorexic self-help group and the parent group faltered and were temporarily stopped. In our early days the leaders of these groups were those who were still struggling with the illness and were too close to the problem to help others. Also, we discovered that meeting weekly was too intense and many refused to seek professional help. We modified the format very soon after that, and it has continued successfully up until today. We now meet once a month for about one and a half hours. The anorexic/bulimic group is now led by a *recovered* anorexic/bulimic and a mental health professional. We urge all to receive psychiatric and medical care, but it is not mandatory for attendance in the group. The family group for parents, spouses, and siblings is led by a parent of a recovered anorexic/bulimic and a mental health professional. The other family members are encouraged to go for some form of therapy as well.

The self-help group for anorexics and bulimics consists of about forty to fifty women. One or two men will come on occasion. We break into two groups, each with two leaders. The members are encouraged to talk about their frustrations in coping with their problems with family members, friends, jobs, etc. The recovered AN/B suggests that they limit their discussion about the symptoms because that's not actually where the problem lies. Many (even the leaders) will say that for years they thought that food was the problem. Very often it is difficult to bring the topics to a feeling level, so masked are the anxieties about everyday challenges.

These groups are adjuncts to medical and psychiatric care and are not to be used as a substitute. Since we revised our format in the fall of 1978, we have continued the policy of urging our members to receive medical and psychiatric care, but have not made it a requirement for membership.

The recovered anorexic/bulimic is the role model for the group. She is there to offer hope and is also able to confront in ways more acceptable to the group than if the professional tried. The professional is there as a person experienced in group dynamics, whose role is that of a facilitator.

The parents, spouse, and siblings group meet in an auditorium and number from seventy to ninety persons every meeting. Efforts to break into smaller groups have met with resistance. Members exchange information about management problems, resources, and insurance problems. They express the anguish, fear, and anger evoked by this condition. The co-leaders in the group are more active verbally than in the A/B group. The parents of the recovered A/B also can offer hope that people can recover. The leaders tell the group that this illness is family related and that they have to look beyond guilt and blame and learn to find ways to cope. The family members are encouraged to look at what is happening within the family that may be contributing to and perpetuating this problem.

Our general meetings are held on the same day as our self-help meetings. They are open to the public; professionals usually attend for educational purposes. There are usually lectures by eminent persons from all over the world. They have willingly contributed their free time to assist us with our educational goals. Professor Arthur Crisp, distinguished author of the book *Anorexia Nervosa: Let Me Be* and psychiatrist specializing in AN, St. George's Hospital School of Medicine, London, came to speak to us and to observe our groups. We are most fortunate to have world-renowned researchers nearby who have contributed their time to educate us. Among them are Hans Huebner, M.D., New York Hospital, Cornell Medical Center; Jack Katz, M.D., Montefiore Hospital, Bronx, New York; Elliot Gursky, M.D., Philadelphia Child Guidance Clinic, Pennsylvania; Katherine Halmi, M.D., New York Hospital, Cornell Medical Center at White Plains, New York; Alexander Lucas, M.D., Mayo Clinic, Rochester, Minnesota; and John Atchley, M.D., AA/BA President.

Authors, such as Aimee Liu, *Solitaire*, Rebecca Josephs, *Early Disorder*, and Steven Levenkron, *The Best Little Girl in the World* and *Treating and Overcoming Anorexia Nervosa*, came to talk about their books. Mr. Levenkron, noted clinician, also spoke of his work with anorexics.

Twice a year we devote our general meetings to communication workshops. We separate family members into different groups. In this manner a parent from one family can share with anorexics from another family. Often they can relate to each other about matters they are hesitant to share with their own families. They are then encouraged to share what they have learned with their own families after these meetings. It is always intense and extremely relieving. Professionals cannot attend self-help meetings, but the communication workshops offer them an opportunity to listen and learn first hand what others are experiencing.

We also have a newsletter that includes summaries of our meetings, book reviews, current research projects, and, in addition, letters and poems written by the sufferers themselves. They are able to correspond with Nancy, a recovered anorexic/bulimic. Anorexics and bulimics may telephone Trish, also recovered, who is available at our office one day every week.

Board members and staff persons are available as part of our speakers' bureau and our outreach program contacts high schools and universities to ask that we be allowed to speak to students and faculty.

In December 1980 board member and parent Lynn MacGregor presented the board with the idea of writing a book for parents with parents' participation. At the same time another parent, Sheila

Freed, urged that a book be written by and for families. Until now few professionals have paid significant attention to their anguish and frustration. We thought the time had come for family members to express themselves.

As many as three hundred and fifty families have helped to make this endeavor possible. Those who live near our headquarters came to one of our five taped sessions, others assisted through taped telephone interviews from places as far away as California, and still others helped by returning our questionnaires with their specific comments. Anorexics and bulimics volunteered to participate in a tape session, too, thus rounding out our report of what it's like to live through this experience, either as the sufferer or a family member. We thank each and every one of you who have made this book and this organization possible.

WHEN WILL WE LAUGH AGAIN?
Living and Dealing with Anorexia Nervosa and Bulimia

Although real people have contributed real experiences to this book, names and identifying materials have been rearranged and disguised so that families may remain anonymous.

1

Trish

"It takes a very long time. . . . No, it doesn't do any good to force her . . . You do have reason to be worried—but she will find a way not to eat . . . She feels she is fat . . . that is usually the way . . . Anorexics do not see themselves the way others do—they feel enormous . . . Just a minute, the other phone is ringing. I'll be right back."

Trish, dark-eyed and with tousled hair, moves quickly, energy level near hyper but not quite. In a moment she is back.

"I'll give you a list of people who would be helpful to you—Yes, around where you live, if I can." She plows through a list compiled by the American Anorexia/Bulimia Association.

"Some people do get better on their own—a small number. It's chancey though—you run a great risk if you don't get medical and psychological help."

Trish listens carefully, just a bit of impatience showing in the tapping of her finger. She comments with her hand over the mouthpiece, "It's so hard for them to believe that this isn't just stubbornness."

Then, to the phone again, "You may want to come to the association's self-help meetings where you will meet other families—fathers, mothers, sisters, brothers, and even husbands and wives who are going through the same thing as you are. . . ."

After she recounts the details of time and place, she pushes her chair back from her desk, runs a hand through her hair, and sighs,

"I was up until all hours with the club—and it looks as though it's going to be like that for awhile—which is super." In her spare time she and her fiancé own and manage a jazz club and restaurant.

"If these parents could only see that the person who has anorexia has to acknowledge it as the first step to getting better! Then you admit a reality that you've denied before. After that, there's a possibility of change."

The phone rings again. A young woman asks timidly about the American Anorexia/Bulimia Association. She thinks she has a "touch" of anorexia, or maybe bulimia, but she is not sure. No one knows she's calling, but she read about AA/BA in the paper. Her "way" isn't like not eating at all.

"What is it like?" Trish asks. The young caller is very afraid of gaining weight, but she eats . . . "sometimes a lot, and I can't stop. . . . Well, I throw up. Two or three times a day, sometimes more."

This time Trish presses. "Get yourself to a doctor . . . It doesn't matter what you call it, anorexia, bulimia, or both—well, you need to have a thorough examination. There are some doctors who know about it, yes. But you have to tell the doctor. Believe me, I know it's frightening, and, yes, humiliating, too. If you want to get better, you have to have medical and psychological help. I'll send you our newsletter and brochure.

"There are others who suffer the way you do. . . . When you come to the self-help group for anorexics and bulimics you will meet them. Some are nearly recovered, some are not eating, some eat and throw up—or do other things. . . . Yes, it is not easy to talk about. You can just sit and listen if you want."

Finally Trish has a moment to herself, there in the American Anorexia/Bulimia Association office, where she answers the phones one day a week.

Seen across the desk, she seems an intense person, a bit harried but exuberant, too. Sometimes she appears at rest, as if she had come to a clearing, where she is alone and calm. She talks about herself and why she is here.

She is an artist. "I come by it naturally. My dad is an artist, too." She has a master's degree in child psychology. "It comes in handy now when I talk with anorexics, bulimics, and their families on the phone. I co-lead meetings, too, every once in awhile. But I can't devote my life to anorexia—I have an active life—my job is demanding."

But at the age of sixteen Patricia did devote her life to self-induced starvation and spent a number of years thereafter coming back into the world.

Tilting back in her chair, she laughs, "What a change—it wasn't always like this!"

She sits upright. "Do you know that at the age of seventeen when I was at the height of my anorexia, I weighed sixty-nine pounds? And I am 5′4″ tall! I'm lucky—or, no—it wasn't luck. I worked long and hard to get better. I just went back to my psychiatrist. Every once in awhile I check in, you know. We both agree—I'm recovered! That's a beautiful word—and sounds like beautiful music—and feels even better.

"Looking back on it, I can guess at causes—perhaps those guesses are valid. They are for me anyway. But the one thing that I've learned through a lot of therapy is that my inner privacy is precious. Sure, I could talk about my family—me—but it's over—I struggle, but I live. And love living.

"As I see it—there are stages. I think about it when I talk to people on the phone, and when I help Estelle—she's the founder and executive director—answer letters from all over the country.

"There's the beginning—the *onset*. That could be years—or your whole previous life! Anyway, that's important, and you spend a lot of time afterwards in therapy thinking it over. I guess you'd call it rethinking—because one comes up sometimes with different views about what happened or how you felt.

"Then, there's *labeling*. I mean self-labeling, as well as being labeled by others. It takes a long time to admit to the fact that you're caught—that you can't get out of it—the compulsion to starve yourself has taken over."

She counts off the other stages on her fingers, "*Depression*, because you can't deny it so much now because you realize you're a slave to your defenses: *motivation to change*, that's big. People—parents, friends, doctors, therapists—help you from the outside, but the real motivation to change has to come from the inside—from your guts: *depression*—yes again, because now you've got to work on those problems that aren't so hidden anymore. And then the *recovery* process. That means retrieving your natural sensations again—of hunger, thirst, fatigue. It means developing social skills, relearning etiquette, communication, and, very important, humor. As for emotional development, one has to dare to take risks, to make mistakes and accept them. Self-awareness is a major task, but it develops gradually. So, the recovery process is tough and long—but the best—most rewarding."

It looks like the best as she sits there, neither fat nor thin, but filled out in softness, and definite in her movements as she walks and talks.

"Now, in that first depressed time, I was in misery. I knew I had to have some help. I didn't want it though.

"When I went to the hospital—which is really in the next stage, motivation to change, I hated it. I fought—made trouble! I said it was a prison. In fact, I was obnoxious, but I had to be. Now, when I look back on it, I feel it was a turning point. The unit was full of people from all walks of life, all ages, and with a variety of serious problems, and we had a lot of group therapy. I was the only anorexic on the floor. The age range was sixteen to seventy, and I was seventeen! For me, this was powerful—to get a realistic cross-section of life, and to hear about other kinds of lives and problems. I feel such a mix was more helpful than if I'd been with other anorexics. It resembled reality more. It helped me to face growing up. That's one of the things it's about, you know."

Leaning forward, searching through a bunch of papers, she selects ones and holds it up. It is a photograph of an intricate wall-hanging in embroidery. "I did this when I was in the middle of my anorexia." She points out cartoon-like figures—"friends"—as they are described in the copy. (See frontispiece.)

"My daydreams," she muses, "hidden probably from all those assaults of maturing. At least, I felt terribly threatened!"

Here her potential self finds its expression—her happy and humorous thoughts not yet used in living, all held in until she could use them.

Trish grins. "No accident is it, that the magazine calls it 'Let Yourself Go Crewel Embroidery'?"

So, it is with Trish's hypothetical stages in mind that we begin our tale of family experience, along with the anorexic's commentary.

As we go forward, we will enter into the lives of several families who are witnesses and participants in these various phases of this baffling illness, usually known as anorexia nervosa.

Before we begin, a word about nomenclature. Dr. Atchley, in the following pages, discusses anorexia nervosa and bulimia. You will find them to be closely allied eating disorders, so much so that the symptoms of each are often commingled in the same individual. One may be anorexic with or without bulimic behavior, and one may suffer from bulimia (i.e., given to excessive severe binging and in most cases purging) without ever having been anorexic, or even severely emaciated. There are differences, of course, and we will talk about those. You will find as you go along that terms overlap. Keep in mind that those who suffer from either share common attitudes: an extreme fear of fat, an inordinate preoccupation with food, and a distorted perception of the person's own body. For our purposes we utilize the idea that anorexia nervosa "is a developmental and psychosomatic syndrome . . . The range of the eating disturbance extends from total food avoidance, on the one hand, to gorging, vomiting, and purging on the other" (Sours 1980:223). If the term "bulimic," "anorexic," or "anorexic/bulimic" is used, it is in the context of the symptoms in the foreground or of varied symptoms.

Perhaps no one word describes the one who suffers from this condition, except in the medical sense of being a "patient," but being a "patient" is only one part of this long and painful journey. Therefore, we may say at various times the "anorexic," the "bulimic," the "sufferer." Most of all, we ask that you translate any of these words to mean a human being in search of vital wholeness with which to claim existence.

2

Defining the Illness

John A. Atchley
and Susan Heeger

What Is an Eating Disorder?

Anorexia nervosa and bulimia are closely related eating disorders which primarily affect women, largely, though not exclusively, young women. Eating disorders stem from an obsession with food and shape. Though no one knows exactly what causes this obsession, evidence points to certain social, cultural, psychological, familial, and even biological pressures as contributing factors.

We live in a shape-conscious society. The latest diets and exercise programs are constantly touted on magazine covers (women's magazines, especially) and talk shows. A book called *How To Flatten Your Stomach* had been one of the longest-running paperback bestsellers in years.

At the same time, there is increasing pressure for women to succeed professionally, outside the home, in fields that have long been dominated by men. Professional success hardly relieves women of the pressure to be beautiful. While in the past women were urged to look good in order to marry well, they are now encouraged to be as competitive and ambitious as men—without being as noisy about it or without "sacrificing their femininity." Being a superwoman—wife, mother, and professional—means juggling a lot of simultaneous demands in order to keep life under control. And for many reasons, food often comes to symbolize one's degree of control, or lack of it, in the bigger picture.

The threat of disorder looms largest for a girl during puberty, when her hormones go wild, her body changes, and, like it or not, she begins to grow up. A large number of anorexics develop the illness in direct response to adolescence, as a means of trying to take charge of what is happening.

Anorexia or bulimia can also be a reaction to an unstable family environment, a way again to control a disturbing situation. The threat of divorce might, on occasion, bring on the illness, as might a troubled sibling who deflects an inordinate amount of parental attention. Though research on the families of anorexics and bulimics is far from complete, what we do have points to a higher-than-average rate of alcohol problems, eating disorders, and depression in these families.

As to whether social standing or ethnic factors play a part—statistics tell us that a typical anorexic's family consists of a still-married white couple in the middle to upper socio-economic class with the father a professional or in a high managerial position and the mother a homemaker, but not necessarily unemployed. The mother often goes back for training or education after the children are born.

There has also been recently increasing evidence of possible chemical components to eating disorders and perhaps in some sufferers a genetic predisposition, which we will return to later in this chapter.

Several Ways of Handling an Obsession

Though people with eating disorders share an obsession with food and shape, they do not all deal with it the same way. Some eat whatever they want and become obese. Some abstain from food almost entirely, or starve themselves—anorexics. Others binge-eat and then get rid of the food immediately through vomiting, taking laxatives, or exercising excessively. These are the bulimics.

The categories of eating disorders are by no means rigid. Many anorexics "discover" vomiting and progress to bulimia. Some bulimics, in order to cope with anxiety once they stop vomiting, resort to anorexia. Some simply eat and gain weight.

Nevertheless, each disorder has its own characteristics and symptoms. The anorexic has an intense, unreasonable fear of getting fat, which does not abate as she loses weight. Her body image becomes distorted. Ultimately, she is likely to lose 20–25 percent of her entire body weight, and while those around her might get alarmed, she will deny that there is anything wrong until she lands in a hospital. At seventy pounds, she will still see herself as fat. The use of denial is where anorexics differ from most bulimics. While both bulimics and anorexics tend to lie to a parent or doctor about their illness, an anorexic won't admit to herself that she is sick, in fact, she denies it at an unconscious level.

To the rest of the world, an anorexic appears gaunt, starved. At the most emaciated stage, she often loses a lot of hair and grows a kind of downy fuzz on her face. She almost always stops menstruating. Her pulse and blood pressure drop. She can get constipated and dehydrated.

In the bulimic phase *appearance* is more normal. A bulimic might be thin, but not startlingly so. She will hold a job, have close friends, and, on the surface, seem a lot less isolated than the anorexic.

What defines a bulimic are periodic food binges during which large amounts are consumed in a relatively short time. The foods are high caloric and selected for the ease with which they "go down" and "come up" again. Bulimics often binge secretly—until they literally make themselves sick with stomach pain or vomiting, involuntary or self-induced. Not all bulimics vomit, but they do all binge, and they do all suffer guilt; they know their eating habits are abnormal. Some starve themselves after binges or run miles or take laxatives or water pills. They worry about themselves. They are depressed and self-deprecating.

Like anorexia, bulimia has its physical clues. Bulimics are prone to puffiness around the eyes, broken blood vessels on the cheeks, and noticeably swollen parotid glands. Some have scars on their fingers. And if they vomit long enough, most have terrible teeth, worn down by hydrochloric acid.

At a certain level, the medical complications for anorexia and bulimia are the same. Both can cause dehydration and amenorrhea; both can end in death by starvation.

Vomiting, laxatives, and diuretics can cause further complications. The regular vomiter risks stomach rupture and, less dramatic but ultimately as dangerous, loss of hydrochloric acid in the stomach, which raises the PH of the blood. The result of this, alkalosis, can lead to a loss of available circulating calcium, a tingling in the fingers, tetany, collapse, and eventual damage to liver, lungs, and heart. The diarrhea associated with laxative overdoses washes out sodium and potassium (as do water pills), causes rectal bleeding, and sometimes heart fibrillations and arrhythmias.

Suicide is also a possible outcome, though it is probably no more prevalent among anorexics and bulimics than it is generally among adolescents. In this wider group, suicide is the number two cause of death after accidents.

Most physical ravages of eating disorders are reversible. Damage to teeth is not, but great strides have been made in restoration procedures. The neurological effects of over-the-counter drugs that induce vomiting may prove a lot more dangerous in the long run. But most recovered anorexics and bulimics regain their fertility with their menstrual periods. Lost hair grows again, glandular swelling diminishes, and blood electrolyte levels return to normal.

Treating the Disorder

In the United States alone, there are likely to be as many approaches to treating eating disorders as there are theories about what causes them.

The analytic school of thought generally holds that anorexia is the result of a girl's conflicts around her emerging sexuality. In order to deny these feelings she must make herself pre-pubescent again, which she does through starvation. Some analysts feel that long-term analysis, leading ultimately to psychic resolution, is the only cure for the illness. Many analysts today use a modified psychoanalytically oriented approach for anorexic and bulimic patients based on multiple theories and techniques from ego psychology to object-relations theory, and self-psychology.

Others, notably Dr. Katherine Halmi of New York Hospital, treat patients with behavior modification, which involves a hospital stay and close monitoring of those treated. Her treatment approach, however, includes additional modalities, such as individual, group, family involvement, psychopharmocological therapy, and other activities that encourage self-esteem and skills.

Another approach is practiced by Steven Levenkron, author of *The Best Little Girl in the World* and *Treating and Overcoming Anorexia Nervosa*. His technique, "Nurturant Authoritative Therapy," developed in his work with anorexics, is a mixture of warm support and strict guidance, which gradually helps them to find their own inner base of autonomy and self-direction.

Family therapy, as practiced by Dr. Salvador Minuchin of the Philadelphia Child Guidance Clinic and others, works on the assumption that the entire home environment—its interactions and conflicts—plays a major role in the generation of an eating disorder; hence the family and not simply the individual must be treated.

Currently, a number of researchers are looking into the possible biological causes of eating problems. Dr. Hans Huebner, research psychiatrist, formerly of New York Hospital, is exploring endorphin levels in the blood in anorexia and bulimia on the theory that endorphins mediate the pattern of restricting or overeating. Other researchers are exploring the intense craving for carbohydrates that for some people may be a part of their genetic endowment.

At Columbia and Harvard Universities, doctors have been giving bulimics the Dexamethasone Suppression Test, which had been previously used as a test for biological (as opposed to psycho-philosophical) depression. In certain depressed patients, a cyclical process involving the hypothalamus, the pituitary, and the adrenals does not occur the way it does in healthy people; a particular mechanism of suppression fails, resulting in a measurably higher level of cortisol in the blood. When given the test, many bulimics show the same results as depressives do, indicating that antidepressant drugs such as tricyclics and monoamine oxidase inhibitors [MAO] might be used successfully to treat them.

How Effective Are the Various Treatments?

In evaluating the success of any treatment program, it is important to stress that no one has yet found a "cure" for anorexia nervosa or bulimia. What works for one sufferer will not always work for another. Dr. Hilde Bruch, author of *The Golden Cage* and *Eating Disorders,* suggested that one-third of anorexics get better, one-third stay the same, and one-third get worse, which is what you might reasonably expect for a group of patients with many other physical ailments.

Still, in seeking treatment, parents and patients would do well to observe certain guidelines. First, an eating disorder is a complex illness, with physical and psychological components. Any treatment program should include the full participation of a medical doctor who is completely informed about the case. For both anorexics and bulimics, a dentist is also crucial.

In choosing a therapist, rapport, trust, and knowledge of the illness are more important than a particular approach or school of thought. An eating disorder is a kind of defense, something that protects the sufferer from chaotic fears and feelings. It is not easy to give up. For some, joining a self-help group eases the transition; it enables them to discuss their illness with others, relieves feelings of isolation, and encourages them with examples of people who have recovered. The involvement of the family in psychotherapy is advisable too. The patient must agree, however, if the same therapist is to see both her and her family.

Recognizing the problem and wanting to recover are key ingredients for any cure. An anorexic who denies that she is sick and is dragged to a therapist by her parents is unlikely to become motivated to get well. Chances of recovery decrease as the illness persists. Early detection and treatment are most successful—before the eating habits become entrenched as a way of life.

Hospitalization must be considered when a patient is suicidal or when nutritional problems become a threat to life. It should, however, be viewed as an extreme measure, a late if not a last, resort. Tube-feeding an anorexic or locking a bulimic away from food may, in the short run, ease the problem, but both must return to the world again, where they are not "protected from themselves."

As to drugs—again, some caution and skepticism should be used. Some doctors have prescribed dilantin, an epilepsy drug, to bulimics, on the theory that bulimia may be a kind of seizure. Though dilantin is a relatively safe drug with few side effects if carefully monitored, it has thus far worked no wonders with eating problems.

Antidepressants appear to have been much more effective. In a double-blind study lately conducted at McLean Hospital in Massachusetts, eight out of nine bulimics improved after taking imipramine, with an average 80 percent reduction in binging. This research, however, is ongoing and incomplete; no conclusion can be drawn from it at present. No drug has yet been widely used for the illness.

Eating Disorders—the Current Picture

Until about five years ago, concern over eating disorders—both medically and publicly—focused on anorexia nervosa. At the moment, bulimia is in the news, edging anorexia aside. There are several reasons for the change. Anorexia, of course, has always been a more visible illness, bulimia easier to hide. Until recently, many doctors had not heard of bulimia and missed its warning signs in patients. Bulimics were unaware of health hazards, and often didn't know they had a treatable illness or that others shared the problem they had struggled with in secret. Gradually, as more came forward for treatment and more doctors learned of it, it began to get the kind of attention in the press that anorexia had had for years. The wide press, in turn, brought more and more bulimics to the surface. A recent prevalence study by McLean Hospital showed that 6.5–18.6 percent of high-school and college women are now bulimic—as compared to 1–4 percent with anorexia. This seems to signal a true shift in prevalence—from anorexia to bulimia—above and beyond the rise in bulimia's visibility. And as public awareness increases, the numbers very likely will too, as will numbers of therapists specializing in its treatment.

Still, eating disorders remain shadowy and hard to treat, and few professionals qualify as experts. Currently, our greatest hopes lie in continued research and the spread of information through mixed groups of professionals and sufferers. Though many small associations address the illness on local levels, we need to organize nationally to prevent a serious health problem from reaching epidemic proportions.

3

FAMILY TEXT
The Illness

The apparent text of superiority read, "I am in control. I can influence events and people. I am all-powerful. My will is supreme." But the sub-text, willfully suppressed, read, "I'm terrified that I have no control over events, over other people, over myself. Everything is arbitrary and therefore meaningless."

SHEILA MACLEOD,
The Art of Starvation

Family members are witness to the anorexic's life, the observable text, but they respond with their own. We process experience in unique ways, in search of making sense of often baffling circumstances and contradictory relationships. When this process is shared, in part through talking with others, common feelings, thoughts, and situations are revealed. When quantified, this is the stuff of social research—when exchanged, the stuff of empathy and mutual support. In human struggle both research and phenomenological reporting are useful to increased understanding.

When the American Anorexia/Bulimia Association Book Committee sent out an appeal for participants, a number of family members agreed to talk about their experience in taped group sessions. The committee thought that families had something to contribute about the nature of the experience. Some drove many miles to the AA/BA headquarters and people too far away to attend participated in a phone session. A total of twenty-four mothers, eleven fathers, three siblings, and one person in the midst of bulimia spent many hours speaking directly with us and with each other of their everyday involvement, their ideas, and feelings about it.

In addition, people from all over the country responded to questionnaires soliciting more information about what it is like to live with and deal with this major eating disorder. Of the 289 persons who responded, most were parents, but husbands, siblings, friends, and therapists answered as well. Eager to describe the daily struggle, people who had never before discussed their affliction wrote letters to us. Thirty-six sufferers responded to the questionnaire themselves, in the absence of available family members for whom the questions were geared. Six people suffering from the disorder were male. Four families answered whose family member had died.

Among the taped groups Jewish, Protestant, and Catholic members were equally represented. All participants were white. Studies generally indicate that anorexia nervosa occurs in middle-class to upper-middle-class families in post-industrialized countries. Our participants seem to bear that out, although there is a vast range of income within that descriptive term and considerable financial hardship is described. The reports of income suggest a shifting trend in that obviously not all are affluent. (See Appendix 1.F.)

About two-thirds describe themselves subjectively as having had a happy family, although there were serious pockets of problems. About half of the parents reported a weight problem, some, in addition to an alcohol problem. Alcohol abuse by mother or father was reported by families in 22.2 percent of the cases. Five of the twenty-one families represented in taped sessions spoke of alcoholic problems in fathers. Many discussed weight problems. They themselves noted and wondered about the relationship of these conditions in their own situation. (See Appendix 1.D, E). Professional literature suggests a connection with alcoholic abuse, usually spoken of as a risk factor, among others, in the family which may predispose a child to anorexia/bulimia. (For further reading see Crisp 1980:32; Garfinkel and Garner 1982:15, 41, 50.) Parental weight problems or weight-conciousness have also been noted as a factor (see Wilson 1983:9).

Work satisfaction was greater among fathers than mothers, although half of the parents reporting generally liked what they were doing, whether it was work outside the home or being a homemaker. Among the participants in the taped sessions, twice as many fathers as mothers were college graduates, some with advanced degrees. Women were generally in clerical, bookkeeping, or sales positions. There were exceptions, however, when a mother was a physician, social worker, medical technologist, nurse, or teacher.

In addition to the taped sessions with family members, fourteen anorexics and bulimics in various stages of the disorder volunteered to participate with parents in a taped communication workshop so that their voices might be heard too. In chapter 6 we learn some of their inner thoughts and outer struggles.

In telling, everyone sought reasons, answers, warnings, and suggestions for those who will read this book. They tried to tell about the bad times and the good, so that other families would know what to expect and would not feel alone.

Attention focused on many areas, following Trish's hypothetical stages or, in a different frame, the beginning, middle, and, in some instances, the positive ending, the "recovery." You will find that their views are a counterpoint to the anorexic's experience, adding a related but independent theme. You will see how they characterize themselves and how they perceive their families before and in the midst of this experience.

Appearance and Identification

It can be a long and baffling time before parents realize their child is actually on the way to starving herself to death, and then still more time before a doctor runs down the possible list of illnesses and finally reaches a diagnosis. The sufferer so successfully, at first, hides her thinness and her refusal to eat, and the family so readily accepts her evasions and explanations, that the process is far along before it is detected. Even more insidious is binging and purging by use of laxatives or vomiting. There the evidence is often hidden, until one day the sufferer reveals it because she is so deeply panicked, or she is discovered, which may be her way of letting it be known.

There are many ways in which families identified the condition themselves before the actual diagnosis. In the questionnaires parents mentioned both *changes in behavior* and in *demeanor*. The most commonly listed first clue was *not eating*, but the next was depression, *apathy* ("a despair about living"), or *lack of motivation*. *Reclusive* or *withdrawn behavior* was the third most commonly noted attribute. Other changes listed with frequency were *general irritability*, *unusual behavior regarding food and preparation*, *hyperactivity*, and *increase in exercise*, *academic changes*, and *increase in perfectionism*. The sense of inferiority that was repeatedly revealed was a shock to parents who had felt previously that their daughter radiated confidence in her abilities. Her excellence in scholarship and her love of competitive sports have been a pleasure. This determined persistent pursuit of perfection in everything that was developing now was a gross distortion of what had been an exemplary trait before. Whatever the different manifestations, common to all was the *wearing away of that look of self-confidence and comfortableness that the child presented before*.

JILL: She was fourteen and a very vivacious, gregarious, charming young girl. I remember distinctly the day I first noted anything. I was folding laundry and I heard her best friend say, "Oh, Deenie, you're no fun anymore. You never want to do anything." I just went on folding laundry. But about two days later, at the beach on a suddenly warm June weekend, I saw her in her bathing suit. I almost passed out; she looked like somebody out of Buchenwald. I knew she was dieting, but she has a large frame, and you know how they cover their thinness up. I just couldn't wait for the weekend to be over to take her immediately to the doctor.

NADYA: Susie was fifteen. She started mainly with the loss of her period—but she was in tennis and swimming, and people that we talked to said it's not unusual for girls who play sports to stop menstruating. I didn't realize she had lost that much weight though. Then her brother came home from college and said, "My God, she looks like she lost more weight."

CARLINA: Ruth was eleven at the time—had always been chubby—and she started dieting. But it seemed as though the child really was simply starting to develop physically. By September she weighed seventy-five pounds—from ninety-five pounds . . . The thing that bothered us most was the *depression*. She was always very quiet, but she had friends, enjoyed doing things, and now she was sitting around doing nothing—not talking to anybody. So we took her to our own family doctor.

ELAINE: When Connie was about fourteen the family went away on a camping trip. We all came back a few pounds heavier. We all talked about dieting and her father remarked on her being overweight. When she heard it, she started dieting.

COREY: Well, I have a twin sister who bounces back and forth from anorexia to bulimia. We're twenty-five now. When we were sixteen, she started on a diet . . . My sister was always on the plump side . . . she didn't start menstruating until she was sixteen; I started when I was twelve. She lost a few pounds and started exercising. Everyone told her how great she looked. Gosh, I can remember coming in at eleven o'clock at night, and she'd be doing hundreds of sit-ups and jumping jacks. She got extremely thin. She stopped menstruating, so my mother got her to go to all sorts of doctors.

ARNOLD: After the first semester of college, she came home . . . the wind could have blown her away. I guess she was now in the eighty-pound range, from one hundred and twenty. My wife said, "She must have anorexia." But I had never heard of it. And I talked to Maurie, "The body's like an engine; you've got to fuel it."

EMILY: I think Jenny was rebelling against the tremendous changes that were taking place in her body which she was not in any way ready for.

She associated it with fat. She says now that she thought she had discovered this magic way to stay thin, to stay young, to make the periods go away! She was quite stunned to find later that there is a disease called anorexia and that there are kids taking laxatives the way she had for years.

Among the families reporting in sessions, the earliest onset was at the age of nine and a half and the latest twenty-five, the average being about fourteen to fifteen years of age.

Respondents' figures altogether give an average age of onset as somewhat higher, 16.8 years, although the standard deviation, 4.3 (i.e., most onsets are in and around 4.3 years of 16), indicates that it appeared somewhere in those crucial adolescent years, depending upon circumstance and bodily maturation. When the anorexic/bulimic reported herself, the age of onset was older, 19.48 years with a standard deviation of 6.35.

Strikingly, bulimics alone, as designated in the questionnaires from family members, are reported as having an average age at onset of 17.65, and in self-reports, once again, the age given is higher, 21.4.

Professional literature reports similar figures (Sours 1980:269–71; Crisp 1980:23). If anorexia nervosa and its related disorder, bulimia, are thought of as a massive effort to contend with growing up physically and mentally, we would expect that ages might well vary but cluster around those significant junior high and high school years and into the early years of college or working. (For further reading see Sours 1980:222; Palazzoli 1978:72; Garfinkel and Garner 1982:3–46, 25–27.)

In seeking diagnosis and treatment families took various routes.

ELAINE: Since I had training as a psychologist, I was aware immediately that there was a problem and I feared that it might be anorexia. First I took her to an internist who yelled at her and gave her periactin, hoping to stimulate her appetite, and she refused to take it. So then I took her to a psychiatrist who said that she just needed to have some fun during the summer and by the fall things might be better. That didn't help. In the fall I took her to a gynecologist who thought there might be a hormonal problem, so he started hormone therapy for several months. This proved fruitless . . . She kept on losing weight. Several months later she did end up in the hospital. By that time her weight had dropped from ninety-seven to seventy-seven pounds.

COREY: One gynecologist told my mother that my twin was probably pregnant because she wasn't menstruating. Finally my mother went to a Catholic Family Agency and got her into a hospital.

EMILY: I saw changes in Jenny, but I kept saying everything is all right, everything's going to be fine. Otherwise she might have gotten help earlier. It's easy to deny because anorexics are tremendously deceitful and manipulative. Jenny hid what she was doing. She wouldn't eat with us because she "had just eaten at a friend's house." I accepted all her lies and excuses and deceit because she was a truthful child—my daughter doesn't lie. Well, she *was* lying, and I don't know if I was just naive or just using that as, "Good, she has just told me what I wanted to hear; she's okay."

HELGA: Bonnie read an article in a magazine that said, "This is the way some runners maintain their weight." Well, I respected my daughter, an ideal person, to such a degree that I thought she would think, "Isn't that a dumb thing for that person to do?" She gave me several openings where I should have been more alert. I think I was just too blind or accepting or something, but I just totally did not suspect anything . . . except in an underneath, intuitive feeling. I would feel that she's a little crabby now and then, so I felt possibly there's something wrong with her—and I'm a hospital dietitian—so I thought, take her to the doctor. So I did. No one ever picked it up except, oh, that she might have a little something, she has swollen glands, so they'd give her an antibiotic. But they never, ever asked anything specific about bulimia or anorexia.
NETTIE: How *did* it come out?
BONNIE (the daughter): Well, I had been going to a therapist since I was in tenth grade. My parents had started to go to a marriage or family counselor. We kids came in once and the therapist saw that I was depressed. And then I started going to him and we talked about getting along with my family and the depression and stuff. But I didn't tell him until November of my senior year. And then in February I was real depressed and decided to stop going to him. I didn't feel I was getting better. When I stopped, he felt he should tell my parents, so that's how they found out.

EMILY: Bonnie, when you binged, then you would eat a lot and then vomit, did you always clean the bathroom so that your parents wouldn't know? Did you ever leave signs?
BONNIE: Well, I always tried very hard not to.
HELGA (Bonnie's mother): Well, my only thought was that I knew you had trouble with constipation sometimes and so I knew that possibly she's taken a laxative or something.
BONNIE: I always cleaned up pretty well.

JILL: When I took Deenie to the doctor he said, "Oh, Jill, you mustn't fuss about eating," and I said, "I've never fussed about my children eating and you know it." Anyway after five months of hell, of being told that she probably has leukemia—this is so long ago that they didn't know how to diagnose let alone treat anorexia nervosa—they finally said that she had anorexia nervosa.

ROSE: I happened to see a record of a doctor who told me not to worry about her weight at that time. She was 5′8″ and weighed ninety-one pounds and she was dieting and it said "mild anorexia." Well, I hate to think, you know, how I would have lived through *severe* anorexia!

What Were They Like Before?

Are the anorexics and the bulimics all alike? So often, when a profile is given, parents bristle at the over-simplified picture. They do not always find their child in that overall description—but often bits and pieces fit.

LAURA: She was just there, unassuming, doing, doing, doing for everyone, never made any waves.

EMILY: In our case, it's our younger daughter who was the good one—who never gave us any trouble—who was placid. Jenny, the anorexic, was not an easy child—from the day she was born—poor eater, poor sleeper, hyper-alert. But she excelled at things—was talented—very precocious.

BONNIE (anorexic in bulimic state): . . . and my sister was more well-behaved than me!

JANE: . . . and I wouldn't say that my Karly was the good one either. If anyone could have predicted, her sister would have been more of a candidate for it. Karly was younger—always had lots of friends. She was the leader in her group; she was very outgoing.

KATE: My Rachel was everything I've read on the child most likely to get this. She never gave me a problem—she was a high achiever and a perfectionist.

SARAH: There has always been a problem with Mary—an emotional problem from Day 1. She was diagnosed as autistic. We had many trying years. The only time she would be content as a baby was to be put into her room by herself. I would wait, stand the screaming, then finally—this is the guilt I'm carrying—put her in her room.
NETTIE: How long was it before she could be comfortable other places?
SARAH: Oh, when she was seven or eight, I guess.
JILL: Then perhaps she wasn't autistic.
SARAH: Well, then the pediatrician turned it around and said, "Oh, she's really coming out of this—you must be doing something right, Mother." The ironic part of this is that the psychiatrist who had seen her at the age of eighteen months once again saw her at the age of seventeen to diagnose her as anorexic!
BOB: I always thought my daughter was the most gorgeous, beautiful thing in the world and the most intelligent . . .

There were the ones who wanted always to be the honor student, to be the lead in plays, to be in the "number one spot." For the most part the anorexics were "special" in the family as seen now, in retrospect, some having been beset by emotional problems since infancy, but others exhibiting a conforming, accommodating, pleasing, helpful, and non-demanding demeanor.

One mother observes that she knew when her other children were bothered about something; one would whine, the other would scream. But the anorexic-to-be daughter never complained. Many other parents agree. Some speak of the *quietness* and the quality of "*taking in*" the emotional atmosphere. Almost all speak of the *sensitivity* of the child who later on became the sufferer. "She is supersensitive—she has antennae. She can pick up an aura of a situation that hasn't even begun." In fact, this daughter sensed her mother's troubles and took care of her during a stress-filled time. That special quality is felt by many, especially by mothers. The little girls sense, feel, or absorb the stress—the unhappy time. They require little attention and some become mothers to their mothers. Later the same quality of taking care becomes one factor when they are anorexic.

What Are They Like During Their Illness?

The changes in behavior and personality are striking. Parents comment, "She is a different person." There are sudden shifts in mood. The quiet, resourceful, helpful child is irritable, clinging sometimes, claiming total independence at other times. Rationality and logic seem to have taken a holiday. There is misery where there was liveliness. There is no laughter. It is as if she were a person possessed.

CORINNE: Well, as my daughter explains it to me now, she said it was a compulsion; that she could not stop herself. It was in the early stages, and she would do 150 sit-ups and then she would do fifty more in case she hadn't done enough. She would come home and jump over the picnic bench fifty times, and it wasn't really to lose weight. She just couldn't help herself. It was this other person inside of her telling her to do this.

All the behavior now, as described by Dr. Atchley in chapter 2, is geared to the avoidance of becoming fat. Obsessive exercise and other compulsive rituals are part of the illness. The "nice" child becomes a tyrant just as an infant unknowingly dominates the household.

Families are frightened and they are surprised. In the midst of fear that their loved one may die, they have to deal with behavior which most have never encountered before in the intimate circle of the family. They are subject to manipulation by their children, to temper tantrums and subterfuge to some degree.

Our families reflect and bear out Professor Arthur Crisp's observation:

It is a grave error at this stage to attempt to evaluate the patient's potential personality on the basis of her current behaviour and experience of this. This latter is predominantly driven by the posture of starvation which is common to all anorexics and indeed to all starved people. Experience is universally reduced to problems of ingestion which must never be construed as symbolically reflecting previous family relationships, especially with the mother. The only surviving element of previous personality development still within the starved anorectic will be expressed in terms of the balance between her ritualized restraint of eating on the one hand and her "acting out" binging and vomiting on the other hand. (Crisp 1980:92)

EVA: I find something with her that bugs the hell out of me and I can't understand why she does it. She hides food. She knew we wanted her to eat and she would starve all day and then go into her bedroom and binge at night and throw it up. The interesting thing is that she leaves all the garbage in her wastebasket. A couple of weeks ago—I said to her, "Just because I don't say anything to you, that doesn't mean that I'm not aware," and I said, "Frankly, you want me to know, because if you didn't want me to know, you would empty your damn wastebasket yourself and not leave it for me."

BOB: She can sell you the greatest bill of goods, promise you the world; this is it, "Believe me," and so forth and, "I know I'm not any good and I'm destroying the family," and then revert right back as though—they just forget what they say.

ROSE: Well, they think they're independent but they're not really. On the surface my daughter is a beautiful girl and you would think she had it all together, which I always thought she did. She's very immature the way she relates to the household. Her self-image is very poor; I can see that. At twenty-six she has no self-confidence. I would say, underneath this veneer, that she's kind of an arrested person, who may be age sixteen now. I hate to think of her becoming chronically sixteen.

NADYA: Yes, my daughter has a terrible self-image; she's so immature. And I didn't recognize it, either. I always thought she was very mature.

SARAH: Mary is eighteen years old. What were we to do, tie her in her bedroom? She was hitchhiking on the road; she was going into diners ordering, you know, tremendous meals and walking out and not paying . . .

BOB: Gina gives excuses why she's going out with someone, but we know it's just an excuse to go out and binge. Last night she came home about eleven-thirty crying, "Why didn't you lock the door? You shouldn't have let me out tonight. You should have locked the door." She can't help herself.

SARAH: What I can't handle is when she goes on these binges in the home, that it's like an animal has gone through the kitchen—with food all over the cabinets, on the floor, on the table.

ALAN: When she upchucks, we refer to it as nonsense; we use different words, you know. She's well aware she has a problem but is reluctant to admit it, and this poses a thought in my mind as to this concept of this cry for help. If she knows that we are aware of what is happening, and she *is* getting help—why would she leave this mess for us?

Why Did It Happen?

One of the fathers said, "It's in the family circle," and another group member is convinced that "It's a genetic pattern." "I don't think they start wanting to do this . . . they've got the most beastly, miserable lives—lives of hell, and they make everybody else's around them pretty difficult as well. There's something that's forcing those poor kids into that situation."

The Child and His/Her Responses

Parents do frequently gnaw on why and where it all began. In hindsight they can identify problems that were not or could not be addressed at the time. They feel *jealousy* and *competition* may have contributed to their children's difficulties, especially in those early junior high school years, when they were just coming into puberty. A couple reports on their son's disappointment in not being accepted on a baseball team; a mother reports her daughter ostracized by others because the teacher blamed her for revealing that cheating was going on in an honors class. Still other parents speak of their daughters' choosing friends who were not equal to them in achievement, avoiding the students who more nearly fit their own self-expectations. A *disappointing experience with a boyfriend, a lover's quarrel,* or *a rejection* is sometimes the starting point of the self-destructive process.

Brother and sister, sister and sister, whatever combination, may find themselves in a competitive struggle—between each other for being "better at things" or for parents' love.

JANE (mother): Karly's father preferred the other daughter. He was at the worst of his alcoholism. She never got much attention from him. Karly didn't seem to mind, but she did mind! She later said that from the time she was six years old she vowed that Martha would never do anything better than she could do it.

ALAN: There's also the converse side of this. Joanne, the one with anorexia, and I were just about inseparable, much more so than myself and Margaret, her sister. She leans more towards her mother, whereas Joanne—I always called her the son I never had—she loved sports, full of mischief, full of—just liked to fool around. We always played tennis together, Joanne and I, but Margaret, she didn't care for it. She's an excellent child, believe me, but she wouldn't see things my way. She didn't care for school—she knew everything, you know, and this just irked me and we used to fight a lot. Joanne would just sit there and never say a word. I guess, maybe, in a sense I did favor Joanne because Joanne was so easygoing. She never gave me a problem. When I heard about the anorexia, I said, "Joanne, what's going on?" She said, "Well, what do you mean?" She started to cry, "Three months, three months, and you didn't notice? All this time you didn't notice a thing?" The point I'm trying to make is this: If Margaret is bad, she gets all the attention; if Margaret is good, she gets all the attention. No matter what Margaret does she gets all the attention. But good, little old Joanne, she never says a word. She's *the best little girl in the world, right?*

Food, Feeling Fat

The family's *eating patterns and attitudes toward eating, dieting,* and *weight-consciousness* are pivotal. Close to half of those reporting indicated that weight problems and weight consciousness were present in the parents. Thirteen percent of the families reported either mother or father with a weight problem *and* (one or both) an alcohol problem. (See Appendix 1. D, E.)

Food can, from birth on, become confused with the emotions connected to the eating process. Emotional hunger may be taken for physical need. Freedom from disquiet may be habitually sought from food.

EVA: One thread I found in the parents' group was that everybody had something negative to say about the dinner experience. Our family tended to read a newspaper while we were eating or watch the news.

ROSE: I remember the dinner table, when we did eat together, was often a battleground—just picky arguments, that she evidently remembers.

Most parents remember worrying about weight—their own or their spouses.

JILL: I was overweight when I got married and I've been dieting all my life and I'm still dieting. For Deenie not eating was all right because Mom was always dieting.

SAM: Yes—I was vocal about my concern. They *knew*, because I said, "Don't buy any cake. Don't buy any ice cream. If there's ice cream in the house, I'll eat it." I can't control myself. People tell me I'm thin now; I think I'm heavy, you know. I have this body image of myself. I still am weight conscious. My daughter could have gotten that knowledge.

KATE: Self-image is funny, because I was always a skinny kid; my mother thought I had TB. I just never gained weight until I got older, and to this day my image of myself is skinny. I could put on twenty pounds and my husband could say, "You know, you're getting a little fat," and I would think he's nuts. I'm thin; my mother always thought I was thin. I think if I was two hundred pounds my image of myself would be thin.

BOB: Did you ever notice that those kids are food pushers? They say, "I'm going to go out; I'll bring you back an ice cream sundae"—then vicariously enjoy food, in watching you eating. It's so involved; food, food,

food. I was always weight conscious . . . but it didn't affect anyone else. Just my daughter!
SUSAN (Bob's wife): Our whole family is. I have always been overweight and always dieting, up and down. My boys—one runs—he's thin, but he eats.
LANNY (sister): I think it could affect girls in a different way because males are more physically active, more involved in sports. Girls are maybe more conscious of their appearance . . . you know, with clothes and makeup and the hair . . .

ALAN: We used to kid around when my daughter Joanne was heavy. I used to tease her about it, you know, not with any bad intent or anything, but just fooling around. Perhaps she took it seriously. Perhaps I shouldn't have done it.
CORINNE: It's devastating if parents embarrass their children, I think.
ALAN: But it was never done in front of anyone outside of the immediate family, never. You know, we would fool around and I would say, "You're fat," or something like that, and she'd say, "You are, too."
HELGA: Would you say that to your best friend?
ALAN: Well, I wouldn't fool around with my best friend. This is my daughter.
HELGA: Your child is even closer than your best friend.
ALAN: No. The answer is no, I wouldn't say it to my best friend. I didn't mean it as anything derogatory.
JANE: But a little child takes it that way.

Sometimes weight becomes a bone of contention among family members long before the child's eating problem surfaces.

EVA: My husband has always had a thing against fat people. He has expressed this, and my daughter heard this all the time. And I've always been on diets; I'm a real victim of the yo-yo syndrome. In fact, when I felt my daughter recovered I went back to Weight Watchers to pull myself together. She always heard him after me about my weight—sometimes with my consent, sometimes not—and sometimes I could have taken the food and thrown it at him. The point is, my daughter didn't know when he was doing it whether I wanted him to or not. Now this is in retrospect. She only knew that she heard him criticizing my food, my eating, and by doing that I guess she could also think he was criticizing me.

CLAUDE (Eva's husband): I don't think anybody knows why a child becomes anorexic. My older daughter is not anorexic and she grew up in the same environment.

JIM: I teased my wife a lot about weight—a lot. I kept trying to push her on diets, but I never thought of it before today, until you mentioned it, Eva.

Some, however, feel that it is the media that encourages weight consciousness. They decry the continuous spate of articles and advertisements about ways to lose weight and thereby achieve popularity, beauty, success, and perfect love.

A mother, whose daughter is well on the way to recovery, writes:

> What still infuriates me, because both my daughter and I feel deeply for future and present victims, is the unrelenting publicity in our newspapers and magazines and television advertising to be thin, thin, thin. It is almost impossible to read or watch television without this message being constantly thrown in one's face. Both my daughter and I like being slender, but we feel the constant barrage turns it into being the most important thing in life, ahead of everything. We feel that teeners are super sensitive to this publicity.

Another mother adds that girls reinforce each others' need to be thin, constantly comparing, thus measuring themselves against the culture at large and their own peer culture.

Weight-consciousness to *family criticism* of one another to *teasing,* all seem part of the everyday family circle. These are touchy areas, which become magnified when taken in by the anorexic-to-be. It seems apparent that attitudes about weight and good looks—what we deem today as attractive—play a role in giving the anorexic and bulimic syndrome good soil in which to develop and grow. It may be that parents as well are adversely affected by the prevailing cultural ideal of thinness and success, which then becomes reflected and distorted in the sufferer's obsession.

Reflections of the Generations

Family likenesses are seen as possible potential pitfalls, by mothers or fathers—or the child. From generation to generation certain characteristics are found undesirable.

As the infant grows, body contour, crevices, and openings all become definitions of one's own being. The body physically defines where our selves reside, where the other person leaves off and we begin (Mahler 1968:10–11; Mahler et al. 1975:220–224). Children may take on body outlines which parents themselves have found distasteful. Just as mothers and fathers may have wanted to cast off their own physical legacy, so may the growing child want to disassociate herself from likenesses and see her physical outline as her own. Thus, identifying and disidentifying with parental images become part of developing one's self-image. (Crisp 1980:56–60; Erikson 1963:158–179.)

BOB: My wife has a fear of looking like her mother when she gets her age. Now our daughter Gina has mentioned to her mother that she doesn't want to have heavy legs or a heavy frame.
SUSAN (Gina's mother): I had a fear of looking like my mother, but I never became anorexic. My mother was heavy and looked very old and matronly. In those days, you know, when they were forty they looked seventy. They let themselves go.

KATHLEEN: My daughter used to ridicule her grandmother, "Oh, I just don't want to grow up with those huge legs," and she would call her "the big gray hippo." She would say to me, "I'd die if I had legs like that." Well, she exercised—she's an athlete—and the more she exercised the more her muscles developed. She went way down in weight, but she still thought she was fat.

ALICE: I was always insecure about my feelings about myself because I was always very tall. I was practically six feet tall at age eleven. So for three or four years it was hell—until people started catching up. Getting clothes was impossible, getting shoes was impossible. I always felt like an oddball.

As these mothers remember their own trouble in accepting their bodies, they associate with the anorexic's struggle.

KATE: The image of my daughter Rachel dancing in a ballet, fifty pounds heavier than anyone else—I just couldn't go with it. But I should say, "Sure, great! I'll help with the costumes . . ." Sometimes our visions of what our daughters should be or look like . . .
CORINNE: . . . are not *their* visions!

In their efforts to become a person, at certain crucial times, some children pick up cues from special adults, other than parents.

MARILYN: My mother-in-law has a terminal illness; she's just withering away. She has always lived with us. The therapist seems to think that this could possibly have something to do with Joanne being so conscious of the weight bit because of her grandmother's getting so skinny. My mother-in-law had a colostomy—and after her meals she'll go and vomit. Now, when Joanne was eight she was exposed to this. It doesn't bother Joanne after she eats to go vomit. Back then she would say to my mother-in-law, "Gram, did you just throw up?" And Gram would say, "Yes, Joanne."

Often body image and role models are linked together in the growing child's mind so that she may want to divest herself of becoming like mother by way of the body. One mother, whose life had been burdened with many children and an alcoholic husband, muses, "What girl wants to grow up to imitate mother, if she's going to have to bear all this!"

The Effect of Previous Family Stress

Some mothers became widowed during their daughters' formative years, some experienced other losses, some suffered from depressions, and still others were contending with stressful marital situations. One mother sighs, "She saw me sobbing through life." The children became a part of mother's essence, attempting to fulfill her needs as well. Mothers did not seek this knowingly. It wasn't an obvious thing. It is perhaps understood only now in retrospect.

CARLINA: I think I'm probably more depressed now than I ever was. When my son was born I had phlebitis and I wasn't really able to get around and I was supposed to spend time in bed at that time, but I wasn't really depressed. My daughter wasn't quite four years old and I remember she used to go and take her own bath and stuff without any help because of the fact I had two smaller children and I had the problem with the phlebitis . . . So, she was always trying to help out.

ELAINE: Other kids are more apt to complain, whereas the anorexics during these early years are the ones that don't say anything. They accept it.

CARLINA: That's right, they accept it. But later on I think maybe they're trying to get even in a way. They're trying to catch up for what they missed. That's the way I always feel about it.

JILL: Well, my oldest child was very ill for a whole year when I was carrying Deenie and then afterwards. I didn't have time to be depressed. You just don't have time to be. I was just living each day, just getting through. But talking about guilt—I always felt that the reason that Deenie became an anorexic was because of the time when she was little when I would have, you know, been holding her and nurturing as I did all my other children . . . she spent a lot of time with nurses because I had to spend so much time with my other child who was in the hospital. Deenie was the one that suffered the most. I said this though to her just a couple of months ago and she said, "Oh, no, Mom, that's not the reason," and gave me another.

LAURA: My daughter was four when her older sister lost her fiancé in Viet Nam and that was a very traumatic time for the family. I'm sure it had an impact on her at that time, although a neighbor took her off our hands for several days. That was at that same age you're talking about.

He was like a son to us. I did go through a great deal of depression myself where I tried to help my daughter get through this time in her life. It took me a long time and finally I wrote a story about him and that's what helped me most. I sat down in the backyard one day and communed with nature and trees and God and noises, and I wrote that story. I must say it took care of it for me. I was able to help my daughter more and somehow it brought him closer to us and yet I was able to let go. So that was a trauma in our lives.

ARNOLD: My wife suffered postnatal depression with the third child, but I think that's a fairly common occurrence. Anyway it wasn't a long thing—

less than three months. I really don't think that had any significance. Jane was five. It was so brief; I don't believe that was part of it. We've had trauma, yes, but no more, I think, than any other families.

CARLINA: Yes, but I wonder why is one affected and the other—why is my one child different than the other three?

ARNOLD: Well, I'm saying that they are programmed to be that way chemically or it's just the way they are put together biologically, so that they are *ultrasensitive*. I don't know.

LAURA: I think so, too. I mentioned my other daughter's fiancé and his death, but it wasn't she who became anorexic . . . it was the four-year-old who was the most *sensitive* of all of them—quiet—and smiling the least of all of them.

JANE: The years my husband was drinking I had tried to find Al-Anon, but I didn't pursue it. Then I had another baby. I had six children at this point and I was the only person that was doing anything—taking care of the house, the kids, and everything. In all those years of living with an alcoholic under a very difficult situation, I had never gone for anything. But when Karly got her problem, I finally realized that I was so miserable that I went to Al-Anon and *that was the beginning of me starting to put my act together*. You know, when I first went to therapy I said, "I came from a very normal family; nothing was wrong in my family." Of course, this wasn't true. And I'm not blaming my mother or father because *they* came from a family that was just passed along. You don't have to feel guilty about it, but that's one of the things in my family, I suppose, *never trying to really deal with a problem*. Most of us have areas of unresolved problems; and because these kids are exceptionally intelligent, *exceptionally sensitive*, and *exceptionally intuitive*, they know. My daughter used to explain things to her sister who was two years old; they were *feeling* things that she would explain to her, why so and so is doing this and why so and so's doing that. So, in a sense this child was the *bearer of the emotions* in the family and that's a heavy burden for a little kid.

KATHLEEN: Right! We always said that Joyce was four going on forty. She always had an old head, you know, that perfect type of little girl, grade A, very typical. And it seemed at that point she was very worried about *what was going to happen to me, not what was going to happen to her*. Oh, look at mommy, she's crying all the time. And, she'd be starting to cook for me—and "Please, I want you to go out; you can't sit in the house." I went away. Really, it was the worst thing I could have done because I wasn't ready for it. And I left my girlfriend's daughter to watch my children while I was away. Both kids loved her. I figured I would give the kids a relief from seeing this poor old hag just whipping around the house—me! I had said to the babysitter, "You know, just kind of keep an eye on Charlie," the little one, "because he gets into trouble all the time. Joyce is perfect, you don't have to worry about her."

On Becoming Separate

Often a mother's sense of her own individuality and her daughter's are intertwined. When separated there may be a greater feeling of autonomy for both.

COLLEEN: From the time she was a little girl, Annie's been extremely close to me. I can remember when she was really little, a little tiny tot, she used to kiss my feet. That's how much she was close to me. When she got anorexic, I thought I was going to go out of my mind; she would not leave my side. It was like *she wanted to walk in my shoes.*

CORINNE: The therapist would point out to us that "You're both saying the same thing; you're both thinking the same thing." So one of the things she's had to do is separate our lives, and I got to the point in my life where I didn't know who I was. I was Colette's mother and that's all. I was not myself.

JANE: I was Mrs. So-and-So. I didn't even tell half the people what my first name was. I was just so busy trying to keep my family together, educate my children, and do my job.

CORINNE: And it's great to know now that I'm a person and I can do things for myself.

COLLEEN: Annie would do all my housework; she would cook all my meals. If I went to the store, she wanted to go with me, and I used to have the hardest time. I wanted to be alone sometimes, because, to be very honest, you know, sometimes you just feel like saying, "Leave me alone," but then that makes you feel bad because she's a sick little girl. It was as if she would take over ME. She would have *been* me if she could have been me, you know. That was when she was very young, when she got it the very first time. Of course, she started to go into therapy. We found out she was a very angry child. This child, who walked around in our home and did everything for everybody, for her brothers and for her sisters—*she would give her life away* if it would make somebody else happy, and she never demanded anything for herself. This child was very, very angry! The doctor used to have her hit a pillow with a baseball bat just to vent the anger, and of course, as time went on, she got better. When she was in high school, again she started with problems.

She was raised by a mother, me, who was raised in a Catholic school. I thought it was wrong to be negative about anything. We'd sit around our kitchen table and the children would come home and say, "That teacher, that blank, blank, blank," And right away I would say, "Don't say that; that's terrible to say that kind of thing." And I tended to make the child feel guilty for the fact that they had feelings of anger and feelings of hatred, because somewhere in my childhood I was taught that you don't feel this way. Well, that's a bunch of baloney. It's what you do about how you feel that's important. She was raised by a mother who didn't know any different. I thought that's the way you did it.

Well, *my* weight went right up again, 187 pounds. I was a Weight-Watcher for a very long time. I made them very rich! Then I went into a program that I now belong to for six years. It's the Overeaters Anonymous program. It's sort of like Alcoholics Anonymous. Through that program I learned how to get myself together.

If I had to pinpoint what helped my daughter more than anything else, it was *that I learned I had to be responsible for myself.* As I changed my reaction patterns, then so did my daughter. I was able to teach her a different way. I thought we lived in a very happy home, because I lived in a *denial stage.* I felt so guilty about the fact that I was *not* happy that my relationship with my husband was not good a lot of times. But a good Catholic woman with seven children and a fine home and two cars and all that should not be unhappy! Well, I had to learn to face what the honesty of my life was and then react differently and, thank God, our children have changed considerably.

I am like two different people. *I believe that if I had not changed, my daughter would not have*—would not be where she is today. I am never going to allow her to pull me down with her again because if I do, it doesn't help her. The best thing that I've learned that I can do for myself and for my family is to keep myself together, and so when she calls me from school today and she has a problem, she knows I'm not going to fall apart on the phone anymore. I will help her, but when I hang up I know she knows that I'm going to go on with my life and that I'm leaving the responsibility for her to go on with *her* life to her.

4

FAMILY TEXT
The Family

"Not only has this past's future ceased to be a future, but in becoming the present it has often disappointed our hopes."

SIMONE DE BEAUVOIR,
The Coming of Age

When one becomes a parent, responsibility for the care and feeding of the young human being is assumed. This care and feeding is translated into a profound manifestation of caring for another and of furthering life. Now, with anorexia, this way of showing love and concern is rejected and misused, even to the point of renouncing life.

The family changes. The focus shifts. Where there may have been faith that living would hold some joys and rewards, even during other bad times, there now is sadness and wonder. A customary phrase repeated by families is "It is like walking on eggs."

Everyday management becomes complicated. The most commonly listed problems were related to food, its purchase, selection, or preparation. In those families where self-starvation predominated, rather than bulimia, fear regarding the person's health and concern about getting the person to eat was the second most commonly reported problem. When both aspects of the illness were present, *worry* was most often listed as a part of daily life, followed by problems related to food.

At least half of the parents in the survey reported that they involve themselves in buying special foods for the child who is ill, whether with anorexic, bulimic, or mixed symptoms. There seemed more concern about nutritional adequacy on the part of those dealing with anorectic behavior, while for some who dealt with bulimic behavior, the quantity, expense, and difficulty in providing for the whole family posed a special problem that was often a source of anger and frustration. Family members in AA/BA group meetings will often remark upon the staggering amounts of money that the bulimic spends on food. In addition, the quantities of food consumed by the bulimic member reduces the family larder so that other siblings and parents go without or have to replenish supplies at unexpected times. Tension and uncertainty in daily life are mentioned, as are hopelessness and depression.

Fear for the person's life is handled in a variety of ways, from denial of any fear at all (4.3 percent of the respondents) to reliance on prayer (20.1 percent). A small percentage talked with others about the fears, and an even smaller percentage talked to the person with the disorder in an attempt to change her behavior. One person, whose daughter died, stated "I thought it could never happen—ever!" Another mother, whose son died, said that she had dealt with her fear by trying "to get help or get him to get help."

The daily expressions of relatedness are askew, and one goes about the usual routine with a sense of disquiet and foreboding.

ALICE: You're in the middle of nowhere and you have your own personal problems with growing older and an arthritic condition. Working a full time job is not the easiest thing. And then I come home to face battling these two, with the loss of my husband and no one to talk to and no one to turn to . . .

SUSAN: She can't get into anything. She's bored—doesn't want to get involved.

JILL: And that's why it's very hard to take a stand. You feel very sorry.

BOB: So what we do is take her with us if we have to go shopping at the mall to get her mind off it. We get her involved socially if we can, if we're going out visiting someone, instead of leaving her home alone where she has all that time just to think of one thing, food. We try to occupy her as much as we can. But how long can you get away with that?

JILL: She's not working?

SUSAN: She hasn't worked in six months.

BOB: How can they get a job when they haven't got the strength to stand for any length of time?

NADYA: I get the feeling, from some of the doctors that we've talked with, that we may have little horses that are very slim but that they're able to do a lot more than we think.

BOB: It's endless. Here, after four and a half years we're still doing research; we're still trying to find out; and I'm resigning myself.

SAM: Good, that you're resigning yourself.

BOB: I said to Gina, "Look, I've made up my mind. You're going to die, period. I hate to say it, but Gina, I can see the end. You can get away with it just so long, but it has to catch up with you because you're destroying your insides and the internist told you that; your neurologist told you that when you were in the hospital. Gina, if that's the way you want to live, to die, there's nothing we can do about it. You're just destroying yourself and if that's what you want . . ."

SAM: From what you say now you have resolved something. Yet, in reality, you don't practice what you say.

BOB: I'll be very honest with you—I have mixed emotions. It's still your child, you still care.

You've got to be made of iron or stone. You have feelings. You're seeing your own child being destroyed in front of you. You just can't say, "Well, fine, I'm going to watch you die."

SAM: I said to my daughter, "When you finish your education, you're not coming home for two reasons. One, I can't stand it, it hurts me. And, two, it's probably better for you if you're on your own." And she started crying. Actually in my mind after that point I forgot about her. I couldn't really, of course. If she would get really bad and I'd have to put her in the hospital, I would have done something. But to some degree I got more relaxed. I wasn't involved with her, watching her, and checking over her, knowing all the tricks.

SUSAN: She doesn't hate you?

SAM: No.

ANN: I believe that as children there was a fight *we* had to put up, even if we weren't armed for it, to survive in our society then. We had to make our own way, in school and everything. I never went to my parents with problems; I couldn't.

BOB: I agree with Sam about taking a definite position, but unfortunately, I vacillate. This morning when we were leaving Gina says, "Dad, can you leave me $10?" "For what?" "Well, I don't want to be broke and I don't want to be without money." I says, "Well, that's ridiculous. You got everything here. You have a few dollars in your pocketbook." Then because we're going away—this is a big time for us here, just getting away. This is one of the best social days I've had for a long time. Really, with a free lunch to boot! So, just to ease my conscience, I compromised and I left five bucks.

NADYA: We too came from very modest circumstances and again we had to work quite hard to get what we have. With the kids, I tended to shield them financially. Only now with my daughter's anorexia it's starting to drain us so badly, for all the medical care and some of the things that go along with that.

KATE: I've gone through buying special foods and we all go on this diet with her and I keep cake and cookies out of the house and everything. But I find myself hiding cookies for my son in his room. I just can't condone that I can accept that she does this.

MARILYN: I can't accept it, but I've become strong; I don't know why. I'm very patient with her, but it bothers me when I see her eat a half a large jar of peanut butter—at one sitting—and I say to myself, "That's $4.19 that's going to go right down the drain." I keep quoting these because my food bill is terrible. She'll open a gallon of ice cream and eat right from the gallon, and I'll say, "Joanna, would you please take it and put it in a cup or in a dish." But she is too engrossed with this eating, and her fingers will go in the jar of peanut butter, so my older one won't eat anything that Joanna touches.

EVELYN: I think probably the most difficult thing that we've had to go through was when she would start drinking water continuously until she started throwing up. This would go on day and night. We finally had to put locks on her bedroom door to keep her from going down and drinking water.

JILL: Were you getting medical help for her at that time?

EVELYN: No, not really, but we did end up hospitalizing her several times. She would get her body chemistry so completely out of whack that she would have gone into—well, it would be like a severe seizure—and there was one time that she did end up in intensive care at the hospital.

Brothers and Sisters

The presence of illness in the family requires some accommodation for siblings. They must cope with their own challenges in growing up and, at the same time, deal with the experience of a brother or sister who is having extreme difficulty. They manage psychically and behaviorally in various ways.

EMILY: My older girl was pretty good through this, but she harbored tremendous resentment. She was just very, very quiet. She didn't make any trouble, but she resented us all. She hated Jenny, our sufferer, and she resented my letting this happen and resented my husband walking away, but she never gave us a stitch of trouble. At eighteen she finished high school and she left for Nevada and proceeded to make a mess of her life that was absolutely unbelievable. It's like she said, "All right. For eighteen years I was good and I was quiet; now watch me." She's a divorcée, a young woman in her early twenties, who has a four-year-old child and no means of support. But, now she's finishing her final year in college and she's straightening up beautifully. So, in her own quiet way, she did her own rebelling when she was ready. It's funny—they can't vie for attention against the anorexic. You, as a parent, had just so much time and energy. So she waited.

LANNY (sister to Connie, a sufferer): It's a very hard time with this in the family. I found that I, in one way, denied my sister's existence. One day I mentioned her to my friends and they said, "My God, I never knew you had a sister." I didn't have my friends over to my house. They stayed away.
JILL: Because you were embarrassed?
LANNY: Yes. It was hard for me to look at her. In the house it was different. Outside, I never wanted to see her. We never went to school together or came home together. I never saw her during the day, never associated her as part of me. I've been really thinking about it. I want to know how the whole thing has affected me. I realize at one point it

was just too much and too difficult. I was having migraine headaches at thirteen years old. I just denied that it was going on. It was just so frustrating and I couldn't communicate, even though I tried. You take that attitude where you just don't care. Well, that's what I did.

SARAH: I can identify with what Lanny said because my boy that is in school just chooses to stay away from his sister completely. He just denies that she exists. He's very angry at what she has caused the family. It makes me angry that he doesn't show more compassion towards her.

SUSAN: Yes, my two boys, the same way. They said they washed their hands of her and they say she's destroying the two of us. One of them said he cannot feel sorry or try to help anybody that has made this decision to do this to themselves. When she was in the hospital they didn't even visit her.

SARAH: Neither did my sons.

KATE: My son said, "Why don't you just let her be?" He said, "All the other kids have problems eating. Every kid in school is thinking about dieting. Why is she a case?" He doesn't want to accept it.

COREY: But I have guilt feelings about it, growing up and kind of ignoring her. It seemed like she was always tagging along and when we got to teenage years I kind of went off and was growing up and she wasn't, and I used to yell at her all the time, "Why don't you do this? Why don't you do that? Why don't you wear a little make-up? Why don't you . . .? Why don't you lose weight?"

LAURA: Of course, Polly's siblings were out of the home, but they were devastated. They were afraid they would wake up one morning and find they didn't have a sister.

MIKE (Connie's brother): Well, I know it was rough on me because when my sister first went into the hospital I was a senior in high school. I was getting ready to go to college. And when I needed some guidance as to what career I should pursue and what college I should go to, my parents were so obsessed with my sister that I was just left on my own to go do it. I wasn't resentful of her attention, but it affected me.

ELAINE (Connie's mother): The other children, Mike and Lanny, weren't brought into the therapy; the doctors didn't seem to feel a need.

NETTIE: Do you wish you had been, Mike?

MIKE: No. It's interesting because going to the self-help groups and hearing other people talk, it seems like a lot of people recommend family therapy. I went through it myself in my own way, but it was on my own terms and not with the therapy. The important thing is to deal with it. My sister always seemed to follow after me and she always did whatever I did. She always tried to emulate me and then, when I hit adolescence, I kind of went on my own, and that's where the guilt came in on my part, because I blame myself. I stopped paying attention to her and I stopped being the good brother to her and that's why she's like this. Then in time I realized it was not my doing and therefore the guilt was eased. So you have to realize that it's not your doing—it's their problem.

Thus siblings try to cope, understand, and sometimes ensure their own preservation by remaining at a distance from the source of pain.

Father

His relatedness to his child in trouble appears to be a potent and vital force. He may be somewhat more removed than mother, but his significance pervades the family. Absence by death or divorce does not rob him of significance, for the *idea* of father and of husband summons up a host of images of support, love, approval, being cherished, rejection, or loss.

One mother found pleasure in giving her daughter the father she herself had not had and therefore overlooked the extra closeness of father and daughter. Only on reflection did she realize that it was her own needs that were being fulfilled indirectly, not her daughter's.

One father felt his family unit threatened when his daughter reached out to someone else when she was having problems. His view of closeness and rightness may have closed the circle too much for her to begin to find her own independence.

ALAN: I didn't like this swimming coach interfering. I felt no one could resolve it but my wife and I. We didn't want any outsiders coming in there, especially people I didn't know.

MARILYN: And that's when Joanna ran away.

ALAN: Yes. She took off one day for several hours. And you know who had to go and get her to bring her back, don't you? Her coach! Sure, and I was standing right there! I have learned to accept this woman. She's a wonderful per—(he and the group laugh together as he hesitates) she's a nice person. She's a nice person and she comes to our house.

For mothers, the unhappiness of the past in the relationship with their own fathers and husbands is remembered in the family atmosphere, even though the present can offer so much more than the past seemed to give.

KATE: I never had a good relationship with men, ever; you know, my father and my first husband. The only one I get along with is my husband now. We're friends. I bad-mouthed Rachel's father, which I shouldn't have done, I realize now. And she has picked up the same attitude towards men from me, even boyfriends. She's fourteen and she's really an attractive girl, but she's never had a boyfriend. She pushes away from boys, and I wish I could change that, because I know it's wrong now. It's hard not to say that we haven't passed these fears onto them.
NETTIE: Do you all ever talk with your children about this?
KATE: Yeah, I relate with both of my children. We can talk and they know that I didn't have a good relationship with my father. They know what my life was like, and I have said to them, "Well, he couldn't help it, either; he was full of fears." They know, but they have picked up my dislike. Both my children are very distant when it comes to a man relationship.

Fathers, by reason of tradition and the work place, are often less in touch with the nuances of the child's growing. However, they provide and they represent entering-into-the-world.

LAURA: The mother usually is with the child most of the time and that's rough, living with the child. But the husband goes through so much of the financial burden that I used to look at my husband and think, God, he's worried just as much about our daughter as I am; how is he functioning in that jungle out there daily. I look back now and wonder how we ever got through it.

Some fathers walk away because they cannot, or choose not to, deal with the problem of the sufferer and the family. Some find new understanding and self-awareness that aids them in all parts of their lives.

Fathers and therapy of any kind often don't seem to be compatible. Women have always more often sought therapy. When there has been a firm connection made in therapy, fathers feel it to be helpful. In self-help groups and associations, fathers are well represented.

It is evident that in the crisis fathers are, by the very nature of it, involved. They say that they find themselves, among other things, arbitrating in arguments between mother and daughter, the anorexic or bulimic. In the triad father is thrust into a supraparental role over both mother and child, especially where the child has both anorexic and bulimic behavior. Fathers perceive themselves as influential with their anorexic/bulimic children, but, when faced with only bulimic behavior, they are more at a loss and feel less capable of affecting their child's behavior.

The public image of father's influence may contrast greatly with that of his private world, as, for instance, with one father who was named "National Youth Leader of the Year."

EVELYN: And he still has contact with children that he had in the first year he came to work there. You know, it made it very difficult when you can be successful with others and you have problems with your own.

In response to our newsletter a grieving father questions what he might have done to save his daughter's life. She died from heart fibrillation caused by low potassium, an electrolyte imbalance, one of the dangers of this illness.

. . . what have we learned? Love your children even more than you think is enough? Sometimes I wish I had been firmer with her over the vomiting. Then I remember how she would lash out at me when I did try to say anything. I can't imagine being more relaxed about it, although that's what everyone says one must do. There cannot be a more soul-destroying situation in life than watching a daughter gorge and purge, withdrawing ever more permanently into herself, like the boy in Conrad Aiken's "Silent Snow, Secret Snow" into his schizophrenia. What was even more painful to us, looking back on it, was the thought we both had that she was over it—her weight over one hundred, a steady boyfriend, a much richer social life, and plans for the future which made some sense—all gone in a matter of minutes . . . But you want me to write something that might help others. I'm afraid that's the one thing I can't do now.

Everything that fathers felt defined their role in the family and the outside world in now threatened.

BOB (father): I find right now what I'm going through is not just the financial strain—it's the emotional. The things that go through my mind are very frightening because I can hate her, disown her, and then I can care. You're saying now, "Why me?" And all these things that go through your mind are very disturbing. There's no consistent pattern of yourself anymore. You're losing yourself and when you lose yourself like that, you become more confused and more bewildered, which doesn't help the atmosphere in the house.

Marital Relationships

Along with attending to the inescapable demands implicit in the anorexic or bulimic, marital relations can be strained under the burden of managing everyday matters. The relationship, perhaps not very satisfactory before, may now be less so, or may actually be falling apart.

The survey respondents suggest that feelings toward the marital partner change and for a large number become more negative. This is especially true of families who report that their child is afflicted with both anorexic and bulimic symptoms and behavior. Of these, 49 percent reported an increasing negative feeling. On the other hand, there is evidence from some that feelings become more positive in all these categories: anorexics, 27 percent; bulimics, 14 percent; or both 11 percent. A mother, regretting that her marriage dissolved, wishes she could warn other couples not to sacrifice themselves totally to the illness.

One husband of a sufferer remarks that he finds it hard to be compassionate, is "disgusted" with the symptoms of bulimia, and is at a loss to understand why it is happening. Another husband of an anorexic states that much of the joy they used to experience is gone. He gets most angry at his wife, and adds "out of frustration."

Sometimes, under the stress, husband and wife find a new strength together.

EVELYN: It definitely has had an effect. It's brought my husband and I much closer together. It was interesting, though, because when I would get really down Steve would be up and be able to take over, and it worked vice versa, too. Now and then Steve and I have to *remind each other that we can't forget to laugh*—because that has been very, very important a lot of times.

COREY (sufferer's sister): Since I've moved out, things have deteriorated quite a bit over there, and there's kind of a conflict now between myself and my husband because I'm still very much tied to my family. I feel responsible and yet I have a new life with him, and we're getting hit with these medical bills for my sister. I want to start my own family, so it's definitely affected my life. I think it's affected my husband more so than me because he gew up in an average middle-class family with no problems or only a couple of minor spats.

LANNY: I saw my sister creating a lot of tension between my parents. She would know what would bother my mother so she would create certain situations and then would tattletale. She created problems between me and the family also. She was always putting everyone down and creating just a lot of tension and hostility between everyone.

ROSE: I think driving this wedge, whether they mean it or not, makes it terribly difficult. When she is out of the house for two or three days it's much easier for me to deal with my husband who is ill. The unresolved conflicts were there before she got sick, I think. She will say something to me about my husband, putting the idea in my head, long before I even think about it. It's the darndest thing, it really is. Yet she has this other side, "Why aren't you and Daddy going out tonight?" Well, we never go out; that's one of the problems. We have not been leading our own lives enough and I know it. Another problem which is brought out in Minuchin's book, which I was very aware of, was that everything was directed to my daughter through me, and perhaps I was guilty of the same thing. My husband would say, "You tell Myra to do such and such, and now I've gotten smart, I say, "You tell her yourself."

ANN: I think it's a double blade where they don't want to do it, and yet the're doing it. I find my daughter tries to act one way with us and say, "Well, aren't you going to go out tonight? Did you plan to?" I'll say, "Well, no, we didn't." And then she'll say, "Why? Because I'm going to be home?" On the other hand, she'll do things to make us stay home and make the situation impossible, so I don't even understand it.

The Guilt and Anger

It is perhaps inevitable that the suffering invites recriminations. In the everyday struggle few family members feel certain that they are going in the right direction, that they are saying or doing the right thing.

BOB: There is no end to guilt. Whatever happened in the past you can't keep thinking about that for the rest of your life. You make peace with yourself in some manner. Yes, I was overprotective. I always thought she was the most beautiful thing in the world, and the most intelligent . . . We had a very close relationship and she could do no wrong. Whatever problems she had, it was the other person's fault, never hers. She couldn't sleep at night and I would come in and talk to her. It all created an insecurity and an immaturity.
SUSAN (Bob's wife): We always went to school and took care of every situation. Instead of letting her do it herself, we did it for her.
ELAINE: But to change you have to know what the past was.

There may be a way to deal with the past by using the old strengths in new directions to promote better understanding among the family members and a greater independence in living. Taking responsibility for one's own attitudes and behavior means accepting oneself as humanly imperfect. It requires courage to shed old patterns, and it may be that professionals and families need to understand one another more fully in their joint efforts to bring about a healthier climate for recovery.

A parent expresses the feelings for many of the respondents when she writes:

I have been at times very angry at some of the doctors. Without directly saying it, they make you feel that you are a failure as a parent. I feel that most parents are loving and conscientious toward their children, and that all troubles *cannot be blamed on a lack of love or poor parenting.*

NADYA: Again, it's hard to look back and know whether you were overprotective or what. I had to work. I worked from the time they were born and didn't have the chance really to be with them. I might have tried to shield them more than they wanted, you know, a school situation or the like. So, I don't know where the over-protectiveness comes in and where it doesn't. It's obvious that there's some difference that brings all these kids to the same point. I just don't know.

ARNOLD: Psychiatrists are saying that this is a family matter. It's blamed on the fact that we've moved so many times; that it's because of insecurity; of the mother-daughter relationship; or that we have food fetishes in the family. If the spectrum is aught to a hundred, then we might be at forty or fifty in various aspects of all this. But believe me, I see ourselves as fairly normal. Mind you, if we start that conversation then we may get told, "That's how you see yourself, but that's not reality."

KATHLEEN: The professionals who saw Robin did say had we gone through "normal living, without the separation, without the divorce," she undoubtedly would have had a difficult adolescence, but she would not have gone as far as she did. I felt terrible—all kinds of guilt, all kinds of anger. I didn't want the divorce and now they're saying if you hadn't done it she would have been fine. On top of which her father was saying there was nothing wrong with her, that she was fine and healthy.

EMILY: In retrospect, I can see a few things that I did right and a few things that I did wrong. I'll start with something that I did right, because it's a shorter list. During those years that my daughter was anorexic, she drove us crazy. She was difficult; she was deceitful; she was moody. At times I felt rage for her; I felt anger for her. It was really blocking off love. Love was not a thing I could feel. And I thought, what am I going to do about this? If I don't love her she's lost, because who else is going to love her in this unlovable state. I made myself show something that I didn't always feel. I tried to always keep touching; I tried to hug her; I tried to kiss her. I tried to say nice things even though I didn't always mean them. I thought if I stop being warm to her and stop showing love for her, we'll never find our way back. As cut off as she felt *there was always a reaching out*.

HELGA: I think I went through a period of depression and guilt—that I had caused my daughter all this difficulty. Then, finally, I just read anything I could get my hands on—psychology or anything connected. Every psychotherapist and everbody I talked to seemed to give different viewpoints. Finally I came up with the idea, *let yourself off the hook*. You're not the guilty one. This is like a love-hate conflict. The kid loves you dearly, but she's trying to separate herself from you. She's trying to become an adult woman and she wants to be your friend; but in an immature way she has to let you know that "I am independent of you; I'm going to hate you." Well, that hurts her, too, but she's trying in her own way to gain her independence.

KATE: I think I have guilt feelings because I moved out when they were young, and I think I have to get over that. Like when Emily said the hardest day of her life was putting her daughter in the hospital . . . Well, the day I left my kids was the worst, because I was a "superior" mother . . . But I couldn't handle my husband. He was nuts.

HELGA: But you have to let yourself off the hook.

KATE: It's hard for me to do. I'm sitting here saying that it's not my fault, but until I really believe it I can't find peace.

EMILY: Kate, one of the things I think I did wrong was that for a variety of reasons—some of them financial—I did not get psychological help for myself and my husband and my daughter and my other children, and we struggled very badly for a long time without it.

ARNOLD: The thought goes through my mind, well, why don't we just say quits and that's it. But then you still live with the problem for the rest of your life.

BOB: Sometimes you have compassion and then you say, "My god, the poor kid is sick. She doesn't realize what she's doing." And then your mind changes and you say, "Damn it, I can't understand it, there's no reason for it." I don't like myself because of the thoughts that go through my mind that are horrible, absolutely horrible.

JILL: Well, Bob, I remember driving home from the hospital wishing that Deenie would die. I had four kids under four years—then this thing was just absolutely driving me nuts.

BOB: I tell you how I get through it, how I make peace with myself. I've been working since the age of six and I've done everything in the world. I drove a cab in New York, a truck; I was a dishwasher, a waiter, you name it. In a way it was good and in a way it was bad. I say, "My God I've invested so much in life and I'm not going to throw it away. I got my wife, I got my other two kids." *Life has to continue, regardless*, and that's what carries you.

5

FAMILY TEXT
Treatment and Recovery

"The therapist's flexible style can be beneficial to the anorexic patient who approaches therapy encased in rigidity. Some patients report benefits from the simple observation that someone, whom they have come to respect, lives without mechanically controlling every aspect of existence."

Garfinkel and Garner
Anorexia Nervosa.

There are many methods used to treat anorexia nervosa and bulimia. It is essential that medical and psychological help be secured for the sufferer. The two treatment procedures most generally agreed upon as necessary at some point in the illness are hospitalization for the starving anorexic, whether she is in a restricting or binge-purge phase, and psychotherapy. Not all patients are hospitalized, however, regardless of phase, and there are certainly people who cannot obtain or do not use therapy. Among the families in the taped sessions there was no sufferer who had not undergone psychotherapy of some kind. Almost all were hospitalized during acute phases of their illness. Several families found self-help groups to be an important support and help during this family crisis, even though some of those groups were concerned with other stresses, such as alcoholism.

The process of treatment is reflected upon with both very positive and very negative views, mixed with questioning, perplexity, and pain.

Most parents are prepared to do whatever they can to stem this pernicious disorder. However, they feel that the professionals they consult tell them very little about the disease or its treatment. Yet they want and are expected to accept and cooperate in the therapeutic procedures, some of which appear frightening and, at the very least, baffling and mysterious. Giving one's child into the care of other hands, even though partially and temporarily, causes anxiety, doubt, and a sense of failure. At the same time, when the burden is heaviest, one may even feel relief, which in itself can produce additional guilt.

At the beginning of treatment there is usually an interval when the therapist and physician make an effort to help the anorexic without hospitalization. There is always hope that psychological intervention will make contact with the sufferer's own desire to change and get better. It is that tense period of time when the people around her—families, doctors, therapists—are an external *motivation to change*, but they remain outside. Should contact not be made with some inner part of the anorexic willing to let her defensive patterns go, then there are few alternatives to hospitalization at the most severely emaciated stage of the illness. In regard to the young child, legally a minor, parents have both legal control and the customary or traditional right to make decisions. After the age of eighteen, children are legally responsible for themselves and can choose not to have treatment as a matter of right, unless hospitalization is ordered by the court.

To complicate the picture even more, psychological treatment is usually more effective when the patient herself desires it. Parents are placed in a double bind: they are told that it is ineffective to force their child into therapy, yet to do nothing is to watch helplessly while she wastes away with increasing risk to life itself.

During this interval many attempts are made to coax the person into different patterns, as well as to enter therapy. Will matches will; family interaction becomes a battleground. Therapists and doctors are seen by the anorexic as partly in the enemy camp.

Hospitalization occurs most often after this trial period, at the point of acute emaciation with consequent debilitation and uncontrolled and bizarre behavior with the prospect of imminent death. *With proper safeguards* it may well be worth attempting to help the anorexic before trying hospitalization. There are some who do "take hold" without hospitalization and start the long road to recovery.

A little more than half of the families answering our query reported that hospitalization had occurred. Of these, a higher percentage of anorexics were hospitalized, although at least 24 percent of bulimics were also treated in the hospital. Of those who described their sufferer as having both anorexic and bulimic symptoms, 69 percent were hospitalized (see Appendix 1.A).

Going away to summer camp, to boarding school, or any separation of that sort is a most significant emotional experience for both family and child. But the separation of hospitalization is far more important and cataclysmic than any of these. It can act as a landmark event for both the anorexic and the family.

JANE: When she first got the problem we went from one doctor to another. I thought I could solve it and I can remember talking to her about food and trying to get her to eat. My husband said to me at the time, "Don't talk to her about food; that's the worst thing that you can do. Just let it go." It took me a long time because it seemed like we were making a little headway—maybe she'd gain a little bit, and then I'd be unsure. I couldn't handle it. It was a problem that was beyond my control. She just had to be hospitalized and, if I had it to do over again, I would hospitalize her sooner and longer.

KATE (ANOTHER MOTHER): I couldn't handle that. It just devastates me, the thought.

JANE: Well, it devastated me, too. My husband could not handle the problem at all, so I was totally alone. In looking back on it, if he would have handled it, I might have let him. You want someone else to handle it for you. I was extremely close to this child. From the very beginning she was a very lovable child, very clever and entertaining to have around. I can remember thinking—it's going to be terrible to come back to the house and look at her bed and look at her things and she's not going to be there.

I got her to the hospital and she balked. The director said, "Take her home and come back when she's ready." I said to him, "If I take her home she'll never come back here." I stayed there several hours until she finally went in. There was no other way. For an anorexic like my daughter it was the only thing. The only problem was that after two-and-a-half months they got her weight up. . . . we could not really afford to keep her there and then the therapy was just going to start. Of course, no matter when, it's a long road, and that's why the parents need a lot of help.

EMILY: Jane, when you said something about the hospitalization, it really rang a very, very big bell with me. It was extremely important for me for some reason—maybe my denying reasons—that everything was going to be all right, that Jenny wouldn't have to go in the hospital. I think she should have been hospitalized before she was. Putting her, crying, into the hospital was the hardest thing I have ever gone through, the worst day I have ever had. But she did need to be hospitalized. *It was the hospitalization that did help her to start to get better.*

Her weight was not bad at that point. After reaching a real low of around sixty-four pounds, she had gotten it up somewhere in the seventies, and she had maintained a livable weight for years at that point. So it wasn't really a weight problem. But the depression and the anger and her feelings about herself were so bad that life was intolerable for her and for us. Although her weight wasn't at its worst, she was at her sickest at this point and needed hospitalization.

I wouldn't see it because I didn't want her to be hospitalized and so she went in one night after one of these horrendous fights where she tried to force her sister to eat. You know how they are. They'll try to force the rest of the family to eat . . . Well, my husband walked out, and I cried and the whole house was just hell. She went into the bedroom and started bashing her head against the wall in an attempt to either become unconscious or kill herself or whatever, and she had locked the door.

At that point I knew there was absolutely no choice. I couldn't handle it. Even though she begged not to go, I had to put her in the hospital and, as I say, while it was the hardest thing that I've ever done, she made it easier by forcing me. I don't think I could have done it if she hadn't created a crisis in which I would be impelled to do it.

ELAINE: I think the worst moment that I can remember is when she was in the hospital and refused to eat and they had to tube-feed her. I felt that they had broken her will. But it did help her to realize that in order to get out of the hospital she would have to do what the doctor said and she had to eat.

ALICE: Betty, my daughter, was only there a short time, so really, they couldn't do much in the twenty-one days. It was diagnosed and that was it. Then the insurance ran out. So then she didn't do anything, I guess, for a year. She went into seclusion and her weight was quickly dropping and she got to about seventy-five pounds. She was then eighteen, so we had her committed to the hospital. She was there several months.

She came out and she seemed to be doing really well. She got into a vocational school and she was trained as a clerk-receptionist. When she finished her training, she got a job. It was the first job she ever had and we thought that things were going fine, but then little things started to happen. I noticed that she was taking an awful lot of laxatives and at the time I didn't know anything about bulimia. She would go through rituals—go into the bathroom and be in there for two hours and have the radio on and she became a cleanliness fanatic. I'd go in after she finished and could tell that someone had vomited. She'd say, "Oh, I just wasn't feeling well." Then I would notice that this was happening every day. By that time I had done some reading and learned that she had bulimia. She would go to the store and buy grocery bags full of everything and eat it and eat it and then bring it up.

She didn't have any insurance. So we put her in the state hospital, because the doctors at the local hospital told us that they thought she was a threat to herself. It was a horrible place. Someone beat her up. She hadn't even seen a doctor the whole time she was there. We decided she would be better off at home with us. We signed some papers, taking her out against doctor's orders. Betty said she wanted to get therapy, that she didn't want to kill herself, and she wanted help. She had all these plans and she seemed so rational. But the minute we left the hospital grounds I knew I had made a mistake releasing her.

Soon after coming home Betty's self-destructive behavior resumed. She was unable to work and also began to steal. Another hospitalization took place under an official commitment procedure.

COREY (Betty's sister): I felt guilty, you know. She seems so rational sometimes. You start to wonder if you're doing the right thing by hospitalizing her. But, if you look at the alternative, how she was at home, *you have to trust the therapist and the doctors.*

MARILYN: They had cut our visits in the hospital down drastically, so we couldn't go all the time. She would never really go out of her way to call me. The psychiatrist thought it would be fantastic to break this tie between us because we were like glue. As a child Joanna was very sickly. She had rheumatic fever. So I had to be there all the time; I didn't want to be—I had no other choice. I had to nurse her through these illnesses. So, maybe I did smother her, but I had to do that. Anyhow, she called me this one night and she says, "Ma, you've got to get me out of here," and then she said, "I love you," which Joanna hadn't said to me because she had become so distant and so cold. I sensed something wrong. I said, "Joanna, I'm going to come to the hospital. I know it isn't visiting night, but I feel you need me, so I'm going to take a ride there." She said, "No, no, it's okay, it's okay."

The next night I go to the hospital—she doesn't look right. So I say, "Oh, Joanna, are your hands cold," and then I saw the cuts. She had tried to slash her wrists. Well, I went to the nurses' station. I said, "I don't know if you people realize you're dealing with a minor." I felt that I should have been called and told of the attempt that my daughter made. They apologized. They said it was superficial; they didn't feel it was necessary, but the attempt was made.

MOLLY: Tommy was crying and screaming—a big boy! In junior high! My husband and I physically threw him in the hospital, and I took his shoes. At one time I wouldn't have; I would have left his shoes because if he ran away at least his feet should be covered! But this time I said, "I'm taking your shoes. If you run away, you'll do it barefoot." And I left the hospital—and he didn't run away.

COLLEEN: Well, our little girl was only ten and we were going to a regular G.P. He didn't know what anorexia was, and so it got worse, you know—like a twenty pound loss after going to him—and finally I realized that there was something more wrong with her than just being on a diet. So I changed doctors, to this pediatrician who immediately recognized it as anorexia. And he told Annie that when she came back the next week, if she was not two or three pounds heavier, he was going to put her in the hospital. But she didn't, she lost. Well, he gave her another week. I guess he just didn't want to take this very young child and put her in a hospital if he didn't have to. In the middle of the week, before going to bed, she'd tell me she was going to wake up the next morning and do all these things, but she never did. Then one night she said to me, "Mommy, please, I want to go in the hospital now." It's like she knew she was sick and she wanted somebody to do for her what she could not do for herself. And so she went in the hospital.

As long as it was sort of well-balanced, they gave her the dignity of choosing the food that she liked. But at each meal she had to eat everything that was put on her plate. They were going to add up how many calories that she left on that plate and it was going to be force-fed down her through a tube in an emulsified form. So the doctor gave her twenty-four hours and she didn't eat a bit, not a bite. It was almost like she was trying to see if they were going to have the courage of their convictions. In forty-eight hours she still didn't eat, so he finally realized that she was forcing his hand. They took her into this room—we didn't go with her—and that's where they put this tube down her throat. They forced down her food in this emulsified form, all the food that she hadn't eaten in that day, and *that's when she finally started to come around.*

Length of hospital stays vary. Among those who answered the AA/BA questionnaire, there was a range from one day to 910 days: 28.3 percent were hospitalized for less than 30 days; 25 percent were hospitalized for less than 60 days. (See Appendix, table 2.)

In addition to the doubts and conflicts about hospitalization, there is also the problem of the expense. Considered as a psycho-physiological illness, anorexia nervosa falls between the cracks of medical and psychiatric insurance coverage. Because of this, companies vary in their interpretation of what costs will be paid for by insurance. Some will pay for the period of time deemed a medical problem, i.e., when the weight decrease is life-threatening. But as soon as the patient's weight is stabilized, she is no longer considered a medical patient. Should she require continued in-hospital treatment to ensure the gain, she may or may not be eligible for insurance for this recovery period. There are other instances, however, in which almost all hospitalization is paid for by an insurance company. Some families have had to challenge insurance regulations and still others remain heavily in debt after years have gone by. Though it has been thought to be an illness of high middle class to upper class families, it no longer is so clearly an illness of affluence. Even a moderate to substantial income is rarely sufficient to meet the escalated hospital and doctor fees in this illness, as well as in other catastrophic and long-term illnesses. After the acute phase, there are on-going expenses for psychotherapy and medical care and, where the vomiting syndrome had existed for years, heavy dental expense.

Of the questionnaire respondents, only 15 percent could handle the expenses without difficulty. The majority indicated some depletion of funds, with half of those stating that it had affected them severely and 5 percent reporting that their funds were completely gone.

Among the descriptive answers there were several examples of cost:

"Hospital cost $11,000 plus we pay $350 weekly for psychotherapy." "We are making weekly payments, on $26,000 for hospitalization." "The illness took a great deal of the savings I had kept for our children's education." "$105,000 was not covered by hospitalization insurance." "Over $100,000 was not covered." "Completely . . ." [funds used up]. ". . . and have taken out loans on hospital bill and still owe $10,000 on it."

Families can sometimes bring legal action to bear upon insurance and hospital regulations. One family was actually able to meet the costs for the hospitalized member through a sister's insurance policy. Another was able to enlist the hospital administrator's help against the insurance company. Sometimes there are officials who are willing to interpret regulations more flexibly than others.

JANE: My husband had just started on major medical and we put her in a few days later, on April first. Major medical wouldn't pay anything, because, even though my husband had signed up for this plan months before, it didn't become effective until April first. She had been to a medical doctor in February and the visit had been recorded, so they didn't pay anything. [Rule of "exisiting" or "prior" condition.] So, we couldn't keep her there any longer. Of course, the doctor up there did not want her to come home because she had just gotten her weight up and now he was going to start on the therapy. Looking back on it, if it would have been today, *I would have found a way to keep her there.* It ended up we did not pay the entire bill; they have a lien on my house for a sum of money.

In another instance a family fought it through by way of the courts.

LAURA: Our Polly was in the hospital for nine months and we ran up close to a $50,000 hospital bill, which, of course, comes under the category of catastrophic illness with bills that we could not manage to pay unless we put our life on the line and the house and everything else. So a friend suggested that we sue the insurance company, which is what we did.
SAM: On the basis that it wasn't all mental, that it was physical?
LAURA: Right. Because our doctor said if it's only mental, then it's the only mental illness you can die of physically.

Regulations change as more is known about an illness and its cure and pressure is brought to secure adequate measures for care. Organizations made up of concerned citizens, themselves the "consumers," traditionally have brought about constructive changes in services. At the request of its members, AA/BA has in the past year initiated lobbying and legal efforts to get greater coverage from Blue Cross/Blue Shield.

Once out of the hospital the anorexic must now have both medical supervision and psychological assistance. She needs to continue to work at the underlying problems that contributed to the eating disorder in the first place and now reinforce its staying power. For some this stage is entered into without hospitalization, depending on how life-threatening the condition has been and on the level of motivation to change. New ways of dealing with anxieties and challenges have to be developed. Eating patterns require modification ensuring an ability to give up reliance on an all-or-nothing pattern. A sense of worth and self-esteem will be the desired goal. She will relearn how to interpret correctly the basic sensations of hunger, thirst, and fatigue. She will learn social skills with which to communicate and relate. All these emotional and cognitive tasks of recovery await the anorexic/bulimic.

Family members are often drawn into some kind of therapy, either at their own request or the recommendation of the sufferer's therapist. During hospitalization there may have been some brief therapy involving the patient and the family. However, this is not always available and in many cases the chances of its continuing after hospitalization are slim. The family, when not involved therapeutically, feels shut out, isolated, and at sea about what to do, how to manage, and how to think.

Psychotherapy evokes a variety of accurate and inaccurate images for most people, from "getting advice from an expert," to "talking things over," to "revealing deep dark secrets," to "dwelling on sex," and perhaps, finally, to stretching out on a couch and talking with a silent figure who sits nearby and seldom speaks. At the same time there is a belief that therapy is useful, that it helps to talk. The therapeutic process itself is complex and structured with ground rules that must be observed, such as the hour of appointment, the confidentiality of what is said in session, and the commitment of the patient to talk about thoughts, happenings, problems, and feelings. All this is based on the assumption that a relationship of trust and respect can and will develop between the two people involved, patient and therapist. In anorexia/bulimia, where the person may be dependent upon the family emotionally, socially, and financially, it is important that family members understand and agree with the reason for this process, though it may be quite wrenching along the way, even to the point of opening up hidden hostilities. The sufferer needs "permission" to engage wholly in this relationship. It is fearful to step out of the accustomed circle and speak freely with an unknown person, who is, of all things, getting paid for this special relationship. The family members may have similar hesitancy and feel initial qualms about some outsider influencing their accustomed ways of relating to one another. Parents and other family members will often read up on the treatment for anorexia and bulimia to gain some idea of what should be and what to expect. They say they are often not informed by the therapist. They resent the seeming disregard in which they are frequently held until it comes time to send the bill.

When family members are involved in their own individual counseling or therapy, family or group therapy, or self-help groups, they feel less excluded and better able to struggle with the daily problems. Their increased understanding often leads to the development of a different way of living for themselves. They feel better able to lead separate and satisfying lives.

Knowing what they do now, families tell us that these are questions they would ask of the therapist:

1. Have you had experience with this illness?
2. Are you a specialist in this sort of problem?
3. Will you educate the family regarding the problem in general and in the particular problems of the individual patient?
4. Will you involve the family in helping the patient to change?
5. What will be the cost of therapy?

Less often cited, but important, were questions regarding the type of therapy being offered and whether or not the therapy was part of a research program.

We find that there are indications that families are more involved in parallel therapy if the anorexic is younger, i.e., 12–17. That is perhaps understandable because the child is a minor still living with the family and subject to daily interaction. However, fathers are not as often involved as mothers, i.e., 17 percent as compared to 55 percent among our respondents.

In the 18–23 age group of sufferers, 43 percent of the mothers were in therapy and 16 percent of the fathers. Again, the lower percentage of parental involvement may well have to do with the fact that the older sufferer is away from the family, in school or in a different living situation.

Families generally seek therapy for minor children who suffer from anorexia/bulimia and encourage it for the older child, who is not legally under their jurisdiction. Sixty-eight percent of the questionnaires reported their sufferer to be in therapy. Of those 61 percent felt it was definitely helpful, 21 percent felt it somewhat helpful, with no assessment by the remaining 18 percent. For those whose predominating symptoms were anorexic, there was a slightly more positive feeling about therapy than in the group representing bulimic symptoms. (See Appendix, table 3.)

Those families who do secure treatment for their children report wonderfully receptive and beneficial experiences, as well as perplexing and disheartening ones.

KATE: The psychiatrist my daughter goes to has told me to butt out of it; don't interfere; don't say anything; that it's her problem; that she has to learn to live with it, and I shouldn't be on her back. But I find it very difficult when I've been her mother for fourteen years and cooked and put three meals on the table.

The other night my husband came in from work at three in the morning, looking for a piece of cake, and it was gone, the entire cake was gone. She must have gotten up and eaten the whole thing . . . Well, I couldn't sleep the rest of the night. I know she can't help it. But for me to condone it, am I helping her? No. The doctor told me not to even call him up—that if Rachel has a session with him and then I get on the phone with him the next day, she'll feel "he's telling my mother everything I said, so I'm not going to confide in him." I suppose I can understand she would feel that way. The doctor told me to see someone for help, so he sent me to a colleague. But that's another $170 a week. I can't do that. I'm struggling to do what I'm doing now with her, which is putting pressure on the family. She needs the help more than I do.

ALAN: Joanne was in therapy where she had about twenty-six sessions with one therapist . . . who is very good . . . She brought Joanne along a long way from where she had been. Intermittently we would see Joanne's therapist. She would tell us what was going on generally, but not divulge Joanne's conversations, and she would also guide us into how to deal with it and what to do and what not to do. We would try our best to strictly abide by the direction she provided us with.

MARY: Well, I have my own personal fury at this. If you have a sick child, you goddamn well better be well-to-do and rich, because God forbid *you* have to go to a doctor. I remember one doctor—I am still furious. She was a specialist in anorexia. I called her and she said, "Oh, yes, I can see her, of course; it's my specialty." And I said, "What do you charge?" She said to me, "Well, if you have to ask my price, you can't afford me."

Corrine's daughter, Molly, sees a therapist once a week, and every other week Corinne joins them for a second hour.

CORINNE: We don't go back into the past, but what's happening in Molly's life *now* and what's happening in our life now. It's amazing the number of things that have been brought out, and I find it's very helpful. For instance, I worked all the time because my husband died when Molly was four. She says now, "You would come home from the office angry about something that had happened and I thought it was something that I had done." There was no way that I could ever pick up on that. And she would be trying to tell me things, but she would be hinting at things, and still does hint at things now, rather than coming out and saying, "I want this or can you help me with this?" So we're focusing on that now. I find that it's been very helpful.

Jim and Laura went to separate therapists and their daughter, Polly, went to yet another, even changing therapists when one seemed not to be in tune with Polly's needs. At intervals the parents joined Polly in sessions. Laura learned that she was a whole lot stronger than she thought. Both Laura and Jim feel that the experience brought them closer together. Yet it didn't exactly sit well with them at first.

LAURA: I didn't want to go and my husband didn't want to go, but you're forced into a situation where you've got to go. He learned a lot too, about himself, as I did, and it did help us go through a terrible time in our lives, so we just figured we've got to be here, why not enjoy it.

ARNOLD: From my own experience, my wife and myself going to a therapist was a fundamental help to us. I mean, *it really did help us to face up to this thing.* I would say to somebody else who was starting, for God's sake, *learn how to face up to it.* It won't make the problem any better, but at least you'll be able to live with it easier. But you've got to find the right therapist. I think this particular therapist was extremely good. We got him through the AA/BA's referral list.

SHIRLEY: In our first family session the therapist said there was nothing wrong with my son—he stressed it—there was something wrong with our family. Then he dove into my husband and myself. My son sat there and listened for an hour while we got dragged over the coals. I think when we left that session—and it was a long time until he got better—my son was so relieved to find out after three years that there's nothing wrong with himself; there's something wrong with us! I think that was part of his cure.

Like medicine, therapy often is bitter to swallow, but the results appear to justify the effort. No one combination of individual, group, or family therapy provides the absolute answer for everyone. While behavioral modification techniques are used in hospital settings, where daily activity and intake can be supervised, none of our respondents reported having been in behavioral programs elsewhere. (Groups employing some behavioral techniques, along with identifying and exploring emotions, have sprung up more recently and are modeled along the line of drug abusers' groups. They are probably more often used by sufferers who binge and purge.) However, some report measures taken by physicians and therapists that set conditions to which the patient has to agree. For instance, a patient may have to agree to eat enough to maintain a certain weight in order to stay out of the hospital. The physician, therapist, school nurse, or some other person may weigh her. It is usually felt that discussions of weight gain are better handled by someone other than the parent, who may find it a battleground. The parent becomes engaged in a power struggle, which the anorexic can win only by refusing to eat. Many therapists, too, whether from the medical profession or one of the psychological professions, do not practice this physical surveillance because they believe it may interfere with the building of the trust and alliance between therapist and patients. There are divergent opinions about this matter however.

In some situations a special diet is prepared by the hospital nutritionist or dietitian which the patient can follow at home. This diet will be planned for gaining a certain amount or maintaining the weight gained in the hospital. Such a plan does not take the place of therapy, but is in addition to it. Such out-of-hospital programs are geared to both weight gain or maintenance and to establishing different habits that help to ensure the person's own control of the eating process. The accompanying psychotherapy addresses those problems that have hitherto been displaced onto the eating disorder.

What additional supports have people found for this troubled time? As the participants reiterate, "It is not something one wants to talk about with just anyone—or over lunch! Occasionally someone from the community, such as a pastor or priest or rabbi, lent kind support, but most families believed they carried a very private agony which few could understand.

Some who did find support found it in a serendipitous fashion through another problem, alcoholism, with Al-Anon, the Alcoholics Anonymous' self-help group for family members, providing some direction.

One obstacle to families getting involved in any kind of therapy for themselves is the additional expense. They believe that their primary focus must be to provide adequate treatment for the one who is ill. To do that, the family is under financial strain.

SARAH: I would like to see someone. I don't know if we could afford it. We're keeping our heads above water now with my husband working seven days a week. Somebody suggested the United Way, but there again you have to search out people who are qualified.

ROSE: My husband hasn't worked since '73 and he's been ill almost seven years. And for me to go to therapy would be impossible. And with his problem, I can't see myself going to therapy. I just feel I can't handle that financially. Somehow I feel I will muddle through without therapy.

NADYA: For a few months I tried not to go to therapy, again because of the finances, and I found that it's better to give up some other things and go to therapy, just to cope, because after a while it got so oppressive living with her. I believe that money is really the difficult problem—the drawback to getting the whole family in.

SARAH: I don't know what else we can give up. We go nowhere; we buy nothing.

EMILY: For a variety of reasons we didn't get help. Financial was one. *And* a denial that we needed it. But we really did—badly. Then because of some other problem, alcoholism, we got to AA and Al-Anon, and I got a lot of help for myself in coping with the anorexia problem. One of the things they teach you in Al-Anon is to *take one day at a time* because if I start thinking—which I did many times—all right, you can manage for this year, what happens next year? What happens when she comes out of the hospital in three months? What am I going to do then? What happens when . . . ? what happens? what happens? You can really go crazy! But you don't have to worry about all of that at once. Just worry about today. *I have to take care of today.* Another thing they teach you is to *detach with love.* This person is sick. *You* don't have that person's sickness. You can't get that person well. You can love that person, but detach.

KATE: That's hard for me.

EMILY: Very hard, and I think that people need help in this. As hard as therapy is to get, you need it.

Others found their support in programs designed for controlling weight, such as Overeaters Anonymous and Weight Watchers. Programs that help family members develop their own sense of selfhood and separateness, along with love and concern for others, seem to provide direction and strength during chaotic times. Others spoke of the AA/BA newsletter as being informative, assuring them of a network of families and professionals.

A mother writes from a Midwestern state that she longs for a support group,

for dealing with this problem that hangs on . . . she is still scrawny and underdeveloped at 19. She's had test after test done, which shows that the only reason she hasn't gone through puberty is that she hasn't enough weight. I have a lot of guilt; I would like her to get better. It's up to her—is there another mother who after so many years after treatment, is still worried about her daughter's development? I think only another mother with an anorexic could really understand what it's like.

The formation of self-help groups for anorexics, bulimics, and their families is relatively new in this country. Most of our respondents had no such groups, and the participants in taped sessions, whose children had been ill some years ago, had had no access to a self-help organization specifically devoted to anorexia and bulimia. It is only in the past few years that the illness itself has become commonly known.

One father at the taped session, who has been part of monthly meetings of the AA/BA, commented on the results of a communication workshop with anorexics other than his own.

SAM: I heard one girl say, "When my parents got involved with my food or insisting I eat, I would eat less," and it struck a bell because I always was watching over Connie. Every time she wouldn't eat, I was getting angry, being hurt; so I said to myself, "You know, whatever I've been doing is not the right way; it's certainly not helping."

Parents are sometimes reluctant to admit to themselves that there is indeed an illness and, once having admitted it, it is hard to encourage the anorexic to become part of the group—it is as if that makes it that much more real.

JANE: The principles connected with alcoholism are the same principles that can be worked with the anorexic. An alcoholic can't pull the garbage on the other alcoholics that he can pull with people who don't have the problem. So the same thing with the girls. When they get together they can help each other more.

KATE: I've been afraid to bring Rachel to those.

JANE: You can't be afraid of anything. You have to open your doors and your windows. You can't be afraid.

KATE: I was afraid she'd get more ideas or she would say to herself, "Well, Mom knows I have this now and she accepts, so it's okay now. I'll just keep doing it."

BONNIE (anorexic/bulimic): I don't think so, because everyone there is like trying to get out of it. Maybe a few anorexics still want to be thin, but—especially the bulimics—they don't want *that* anymore. I don't think I've learned any new bulimic stuff there—any of their methods or anything like that.

ANN: They make you feel as if you did everything wrong as a parent.

When we came to an anorexic meeting I expected to see a bunch of dummy parents. I was so pleased at the first anorexic meeting I attended, like this meeting! Parents were articulate. They were educated. There were school teachers, professionals. I sat next to a woman—I'll never forget her face. I said if she's a mother of an anorexic and I'm a mother of an anorexic, then I'm not so bad because she isn't so bad. It's a very odd experience to be isolated with a child with an ailment and think there's something the matter with you, and it's so good to be exposed to a group of parents and see that, hey, they're nice people!

At present writing, it is clear that informal, as well as formal, groups are springing up all over the country. Some are led by the sufferers themselves and their family members; some are led by recovered anorexics/bulimics; and some groups combine both professionals and those who have experienced the illness. As the symptoms have become more recognized, college campuses and health centers have established programs. It is our observation that because bulimic behavior can be hidden for a much longer time and normal functioning can, to a certain extent, be maintained, self-help groups of various formats, mainly for bulimics, have emerged with a somewhat different constituency with respect to age and relationships. Members tend to be older, working or going to college, and involved to some extent in a sexual relationship or marriage.

Recovery

There is, for some, a golden time when the illness is in the past. For others, the ultimate state of full recovery has not yet come, or may never come. Some who suffer from this condition cannot get back into life fully. Holding life at bay then becomes the sole preoccupation, so that little energy is left for other things. Still others have not been able to survive at all.

Family members, who have lived with the illness of another member and have witnessed recovery and the stages leading up to it, begin their stories with "it takes many years."

LAURA: She's coming out of it and it's six years behind us now. She's so concerned now about the expenses she put us through, and grief she put us through, and the anxiety, but I think that's way back of us. We're not there yet, but we're getting there. I feel that these youngsters have had so much growing to do and have tried so hard to get their heads together that they'll come out of this much better individuals for having given so much of themselves, and that we'll be better persons for it. God willing.

JANE: In our case, our daughter getting sick, forced me to go to Al-Anon, forced me to go to therapy, forced me to look at myself. So while it's a horrible, horrible illness, sometimes good can come out of it.

ARNOLD: We see change, but we end up back where we started all the time. We've been actually working at it for about two and a half years.

JILL: When she got out of the hospital, she had long months and years of coming up, but it was *like a pendulum.* She would swing up and then back, but each time it was less and less until now she ended up by going to the university and she's well!

ROSE: My own daughter is the negative aspect with the poor self-image, the anxiety, which is well hidden, and with the isolation. I would like to see her have more faith in the future somehow and have some sort of structure by which to live. Something that will teach her she has some tools to work with. She doesn't have any tools, and I really think that would be my wish for her.

LANNY: I found my sister becoming a much more caring, warmer person—not as hostile and always putting everybody down, but more optimistic about herself and everyone else; just a more caring person and compassionate.

NADYA: I would love to know what is a recovered anorexic? I met some of the girls who are recovered, but I still see some of the same characteristics in them, and I guess I don't know if they are really ever cured.

NETTIE: Listening to the leaders in the self-help groups who are now recovered gives one the feeling of great optimism, potential, and possibility.

JILL: My daughter said to me the other day, "I don't understand why I ever did it." She worries about her weight, but it's absolutely normal.

NADYA: How is she different, Jill? How is she different now that she's recovered? What signs do you see that are different?

JILL: Well, she stands up straight. Really, she stands right up, like this. She still is a very painfully shy person. It has not changed her personality, but she's going to a therapist, a female. I feel very strongly about that. I think women are very wily creatures, no matter what age, and I think they do much better with a female psychiatrist or therapist because a girl can relate much more to them. Anyway, this gal's been wonderful with her, and Deenie's coping with the problems that have nothing to do with anorexia. She's a *joyous, lovely woman.*

ELAINE: I see a recovered anorexic as someone whose weight is in the normal range, menstruating on a fairly regular basis, not obsessed with the fear of getting fat, and socially active. I don't consider my daughter fully recovered. If she continues to go along with the way she has been this past year, I would say in another year or so I would consider her recovered.

COLLEEN: If you were to ask Annie today why she stopped eating, she doesn't honestly know. She was so young when it all started, and I think it was so deep down inside of her. At different times of her life when life's situations were not as she liked it, she would overeat.

Because her desire to be thin is so strong and her fear of becoming fat is so strong, she stops eating because she feels unless she *doesn't* eat she has no control and she's going to get fat. She is a lot better now; I can't sit here today and tell you that she's a normal person because I don't know who's normal out there anyhow, but she is not anorexic now.

EMILY: As Jenny describes it now, as a recovered anorexic, for years her whole mind and body were so filled with this obsession about weight, food, calories, and diet that there really wasn't room in it for anything else. There wasn't any room for pleasure. She would go to sleep with it in her head. She'd wake up with it in the morning and live with it twenty-four hours a day. When she went off to college after she had already been hospitalized, she had already made a decision to get better and she started getting involved with other interests. She found more and more that as she became involved in the enjoyment of life, the obsessional quality started to disappear.

The biggest change in my daughter, when she went from illness to recovery, was not weight, by far, or even eating habits—she started to have friends again and, most of all, it's that *she started to laugh again.*

Being the Mother of a Daughter with Anorexia Nervoxa Means . . .

Forcing yourself to face what the disease really IS, and means, and to absorb the shock that it is actually happening to *your* child;

Enduring the agony of watching your lovely daughter, to whom you have always felt so close, slowly waste away, withdraw, and lose touch with reality;

Realizing that using logic, bribery, force, or punishment is merely a waste of energy and emotion;

Accepting anger, helplessness, despair, and total frustration as a way of life, but somehow managing to maintain control when you want to explode and/or scream—or worse;

Regretting that you ever entertained the notion that it might be nice to have a daughter who enjoyed cooking!

Forgetting what it is like to regard food normally, feeling strange around those who *do*, and noticing how it is affecting your own eating and buying habits;

Wishing that there were some convenient substitute for food and that the word "calorie" had never been invented!

Learning to live only one day—or hour—at a time;

Sensing that you are indeed losing control of your *own* life;

Feeling guilty, and somehow responsible for what has happened—yet not seeing how the past could or should have been different;

Discovering the true meaning of the old adage: "The road to Hell is paved with good intentions";

Accepting that obvious fact that because you have apparently "failed" as a mother (when you always thought you were doing so well!), you must now rely on professional help to raise your child—and resenting it;

Being sometimes totally overwhelmed by the irony and injustice of it all;

Burying the goals and plans for the future which had seemed so possible and secure;

Knowing what a broken heart feels like;

Desperately resisting becoming bitter and cynical;

Wondering if the nightmare will ever end;

Needing, seeking—and finding—God's strength and guidance;

Gaining greater self-knowledge, and observing other family members doing the same;

Realizing more and more that underneath all your daughter's torment and confusion is a very clever, self-centered, and selfish individual;

Learning to recognize the many forms of an anorectic's subtle manipulations, striving to stay one jump ahead of them, and squirming when you see others "taken in";

Struggling to achieve and to maintain the best balance as you constantly walk the tightrope between sympathy and firmness;

Having the courage to allow—and even to force—your daughter to make her own decisions (especially about food), realizing that you can help most by not seeming to help at all;

Listening, listening—over and over again—to her resolutions to achieve control, praying that *this* time she'll succeed—but being ready to listen again when/if she doesn't;

Being patient, no matter how difficult it is—knowing that experience is the best teacher and time the greatest healer;

Measuring progress only by inches, and by comparing what *is* to what *was*—not to what "might be";

Above all . . .

NEVER GIVING UP HOPE, AND ALWAYS HAVING FAITH, that it WILL end—and that your daughter will enter adulthood, and live the many years ahead of her, with far more self-knowledge, genuine feelings, compassion, and strength than ever would have been possible had she remained that "perfect child."

NICKI MEYER*

*With permission from ANRED, Anorexia Nervosa and Related Eating Disorders, Inc., Eugene, Oregon, in whose newsletter it was originally published.

6

In Their Own Words . . . .

It is my belief that anorexic speech (or, more literally, behavior) consists of two quite separate, and often contradictory texts, and that it is only by studying them both in order to fit them together and so come up with an amended text that we can understand what is going on inside the anorexic herself. . . .

An anorexic may tell her friends or parents, "I'd like to be slim," and if pressed for a reason, may reply along the lines of, "so that I can wear nice clothes, date good looking boys and generally have a good time," These conventionally acceptable statements constitute the apparent text of her behavior. But the subtext reads somewhat differently. "I want to be thin because I don't like flesh" . . . My non-eating started from positions of helplessness, of hopelessness, of a barely deniable adulthood and even less deniable womanhood. By the time I had become fully anorexic, all these unwanted or unwelcome positions had been reversed. . . .

I think I didn't mention food in my diary during this period because I didn't want to mention my own eating habits. . . . If I had used words, I should have had to think more carefully about what I was doing. I was, so to speak, keeping the secret even from myself.

SHEILA MACLEOD,
The Art of Starvation

Those who become binge eaters experience it in the beginning as the perfect solution . . . Yet, as time passes the pride in outwitting nature gives way to the feeling of being helplessly in the grip of a demonic power that controls their life. Gorging on food is no longer a way of satisfying hunger, but a terrifying dominating compulsion.

HILDE BRUCH,
The Golden Cage

The anorexic/bulimic suffers an agony that is unique and solitary. It is her very own experience. We cannot feel it as she feels it, but when she can express herself and describe a part of what it's like, we fashion for ourselves an understanding filtered through our own senses.

Families have discussed their experiences. Now, to bring a direct experience, the inner view, which can be so different from that which the troubled parent presents, we have assembled a taped session of recovered and present anorexics and bulimics. Putting feelings into words calls upon unaccustomed pathways of expression. These pathways are not usually used in the most acute starvation stage of the anorexic experience. Yet there were sufferers in many different stages of the illness who wrote to us and responded to the questionnaire intended for other family members. A few who were recovered recalled the experience from the vantage point of years. One woman wished that she could speak with others about it, even though it was many years ago that she had been anorexic. Few professionals knew much about the condition then, or how to treat it. Her parents, holding strict religious views, felt that "to be mentally ill was a sin." Looking back on it all, she believes that she was not allowed to develop autonomously because of a strict, authoritative father. Even now, she wrote, she thinks that "it would be a cleansing experience" to talk of it. One person in her forties wrote that she recovered when her parents died, for it was clear at that time that she had to sink or swim.

Others, who appeared more totally preoccupied with the illness, also wanted to be heard, even though their information was often sparse, except for identifying whether their illness was predominantly anorexic or bulimic or both, how old they were now, and at what age they seemed to develop the affliction. This was often a request for the nearest source of help. A number opened the door to their own prison or "golden cage" by writing about it as much as they could.

Thirty-seven responded to the questionnaires identifying themselves as the person who was afflicted. Of these, thirty-six were women. Nine claimed to have both anorexic and bulimic symptoms, twelve reported bulimia only, and sixteen, anorexia only. Five women stated that they were recovered; two of whom had been both anorexic and bulimic, two, anorexic only, and one, bulimic only.

According to the sufferers' reports the average age of onset is higher than indicated in the family members' reports, with bulimics still averaging an older age of onset than anorexics. For anorexics the average age of onset was 18.8, for bulimics 21.4, and for those with both anorexia and bulimia 19.1.

Another difference with the family members' reports was the assessment of a drinking problem in the family. The anorexic/bulimic self-reports saw more alcoholic abuse than was reported by families themselves: 41 percent as compared to 22.2 percent. These figures suggest connections that may have direct or indirect effect upon the family atmosphere in which the anorexic-to-be grows up (see Appendix 1.5).

Among the reasons given for the illness were: "father was very influential—I wanted to be perfect for him," "an intense dedication to self-discipline in all areas, not only eating," "vomiting to relieve the pressures of the day," "lack of social and family attention," "an unhappy marriage," "needed to control the change from elementary to high school," "mother's obsession with her looks," "had to live with father, as mother attempted to kill herself," "wanted to be skinny and still eat," "problem at home," "couldn't cope with my sister's death and my own marital failure," "boyfriend loss," "from childhood I was the 'perfect' child, and was not allowed to express feelings," "overpowering father, not enough assertion by myself," "lost weight, couldn't stop," and "I really don't know; I was fat and lonely." The most frequently expressed reason was that weight gain was feared and to be thin was very important.

Implied in a number of responses is that of meeting an ascetic challenge presented to the young person during adolescence, when sexual desires emerge and instinctual, physical urgencies are strong and unfamiliar. The self-denial is part of testing one's ability to be strong in the face of sensual deprivation or temptation. Adolescents are usually able to test themselves in the outer world, for instance, in school or in the rigors of an after-school job, a long hike at camp, scuba diving, or a survival program in the woods, and they thus achieve a sense of mastery and control. But some turn the challenges inward, testing the mind's control over bodily need. The ingestion of food comes to mean an indulgence of the senses, akin to sexual licentiousness, if not a metaphor for it. In this sense, one is reminded of Professor Crisp's admonition that anorexia nervosa cannot be understood only or entirely from the earlier infant to parent experience. The biological effects of puberty must be taken into account, including "its own discrete and existential challenge and the major relevance of this for character formation during adolescence" (Crisp 1980:47, 48).

A young woman sends a poem to the American Anorexia Nervosa Association, offering it as a gift of private feeling as well as a search for meaning.

I am hungry
craving
wanting food ever so much
yet denying myself
even a morsel.
Feeling horribly, stupidly
weak and my body
longs for warmth.
Refusing to give in until—
I cannot resist
any longer.
Reluctantly,
I crumble
filled with poison
Unclean
Hating myself
I rage at my loss
of control.
I cannot accept it—
moments go by
as all that has been consumed
turns into
pounds of fat.
An unending, vicious circle—
I find myself

defeated unmercifully.
Permitting it to continue
choosing not to do
otherwise
Not having the courage
nor the strength to
end this merry-go-round.
Ashamed.

ALLYNNORE TOM

Words, written and spoken, seem to be a key to unlocking feelings that had been unrecognized, hidden, and assuaged by eating excessively or not eating at all.

A group of women wait expectantly. Seated in a circle, each quietly awaits the moment of speech, when each will try to communicate her special experience with anorexia and bulimia. Two mothers are there with their recovering daughters, with the group's approval. In the morning they participated in a self-help session with co-leader Nancy, a recovered anorexic, and Estelle Miller, professional leader. They will continue to discuss some of the things they spoke of earlier, but now there is a difference. The mothers' presence evokes for other young women reflections about their own relationships. They will listen primarily; wanting to understand the inner dictates that make their daughters' lives so painful.

The other difference is that the words they now speak will be recorded, so that others may glimpse the difficulties and the distress of their lives vicariously. Whatever may be said here expresses where these particular individuals are in their struggle and in their recovery for which there are various routes. It is a crucial moment—one of supreme importance for young women who are reaching out to be understood and to be helpful to others in a similar plight.

Attractive, poised, and with a firm attentiveness, Nancy, the co-leader, begins. She has just come back from a long business trip, halfway around the world. She shrugs off the travel fatigue and digs into the matter at hand. It is most important to her now; she knows that like herself some of the young women can give up their unhappiness; she knows that she can be instrumental in their recovery. Along with her co-leader, Nettie, a professional from the field of mental health, she will stimulate expression, insights, and the courage to face anxieties as tools to help themselves.

NANCY: I'm Nancy, and I'm a recovered anorexic and bulimic. This morning we were talking about values and how hard it is to do things that we want to feel. I know for myself it was really hard to formulate my own values. One of the key things in getting better for me was to understand that *I could feel and think differently than other people*, and that *I was allowed differences*. It helped me to realize that I am a different person from someone else and I am allowed to think or feel differently.

SALLY: One thing that was brought up constantly was that, whenever we spoke about values, we always spoke about *other* people's values for us. We never spoke about our own values really. It seemed that everybody else around us molded our values, that we had to meet all their standards. Everybody said, "I want to please my mother," or "I want to please my father," but it never came to pleasing yourself and accepting yourself for who you are and what you are and accepting your own values. Your own values weren't internalized. They were brought from outside people only. That's what came up a lot in our discussion this morning.

LOTTIE: I have a tremendous problem feeling good about what I feel, whether it be in contrast to what you feel or what she feels or what anybody in this room feels. I get angry when I can't express my feelings or when I feel differently than the way you feel or the way parents feel. I get angry maybe because they don't feel the same way I do.

NETTIE: Why does it make you angry?

LOTTIE: Well, there are certain ways that you're supposed to think. I myself have always been a fighter. If I didn't like something, I'd say it, but yet I never felt good about. I'd say what I felt, but I never felt good about saying it.

NETTIE: Why?

LOTTIE: I'll say to myself, "Oh shit, I shouldn't have said that because now I'm starting trouble"—especially at work. I'm viewed as a troublemaker, but I'm the only one there that had the nerve to open my mouth and say "I'm not going to take it."

NETTIE: How does it affect you afterwards, after you've done it, and you say you don't feel good about it?
LOTTIE: No matter what happens at work, I am the culprit. I am seen as the one who must have gotten this whole thing together. The supervisor feels that way, and that's reality. Maybe in the beginning I had a hard time projecting what I wanted. I meant to say, "Hey, you can't step all over me." Maybe I came off too strongly about it. I can't project the different feelings. Either I'll keep it to myself and burn up inside or I'll come off so strong that maybe people won't like me for that, and they don't. Not all the time. I can't find a way to express a difference of opinion.
NETTIE: Did that happen with your parents too?
LOTTIE: Yes, definitely. It was "Don't rock the boat." My family situation has always been rough. My father was an alcoholic; my mother couldn't handle it. It was very hard for her to handle, so it was "Don't rock the boat." [She is crying now.] But you have to.
NANCY: You do have to, otherwise you'll never get better. It's really important how you feel.
NETTIE: So it really took some courage to do what you're doing now; that is, to speak up and rock the boat.
LOTTIE: I always spoke up, always, but I've maybe never been able to do it properly because there was always a defensiveness inside of me. I rocked the boat at home, so I'm rocking the boat here, so automatically I see the people in that situation as my enemies and I approach them as if they already had looked at me like they're going to give me a hard time; as if they think that I don't have any right to say anything.
NANCY: But you can change that behavior by starting to really feel that what you are saying is okay and talk in a different manner. That's teaching yourself to talk less defensively and to talk from your heart rather than talking to conquer the world.
LOTTIE: I can't do that . . .
NANCY: I know.
LOTTIE: . . . yet.
NANCY: I know. I know it's really hard.
LOTTIE: I come off to people as though I really have it all together. I have a good job, a good position; I have a lot of responsibility at work. I'm in a position where I have to take care of everything, and if I say I can't do it, they think, "Well, why can't you do it; you're supposed to be superwoman." In a way I made them think that I was superwoman

because I would just keep going and going and going, to the point where I couldn't work like that anymore.

NETTIE: I'm wondering if anybody else experiences the problem of speaking up, maybe with your parents or at work, as Lottie does?

LUCY: I don't even get that far! I almost feel as though I have become so numb that I don't even know what I'm supposed to feel. Between twenty-eight and thirty-two years old, the past four years, I've been binging and throwing up. If I really stop and try and think about it, I'm depressed also. I'm depressed because I think I'm supposed to be depressed because I'm not married and I don't have any kids. I have a great career, head of my department, many promotions, a college professor, and now comes all this bullshit. Maybe I do want a family, but I don't know if I do. All I know is I'm being depressed because I think I'm supposed to be depressed.

NANCY: Well, do you think your parents would love you more if you got married and had children?

LUCY: Well, I think—no. My parents love me and are supportive, and my father thinks it's great, what I'm doing, but they would feel good for me because they think that's what I want.

NANCY: Maybe you're getting a message that they're happy with what you're doing, but they really would be happier if you were married and had children.

LUCY: No, I don't believe so. My father would think I'd be fine if I never got married. I've got my own house and all. He'd think I would be fine. He keeps saying that. *I'm* the one who's unsure. I don't know what I want. I really don't.

FRAN: I'm kind of in that place, too, in that I think if I gave myself a chance, stopped eating and throwing up all the time, I might have to struggle with where I want to go, what I want to do, and how I could feel good. I *know* I don't feel good. That's something I do know.

NANCY: What makes you feel good?

FRAN: When I'm around little children, when I can help somebody. Usually I feel good when I see someone else feeling good. All the things that I was brought up to think would give me pleasure and happiness haven't. Every time I've decided to pursue a career that I think I'll feel good about, I'd hear someone say, "You can't live on that kind of a salary," and the first thing I do is think, they're right, everyone's right, everyone knows, *because I don't look inside*. I'm at a point right now where I don't want to look inside so badly that I keep myself busy eating and throwing up. When I'm not, it's just taking a break. I hope I live long enough to get through this one time. Right now I need a lot of help and I'm not sure how to get it. I need someone else to help me. I don't know who, I don't know how.

NETTIE: When did you become conscious as you are now about this?

FRAN: I've been in therapy, individual psychotherapy, for two years and I think it was over this past summer when my therapist was away for a month that I was able to see that a lot of things I had learned, I could keep with me—about what I was going through. But I don't know where to take it. I guess I want to be able to go on quickly. I'm frustrated because it's not going to happen fast, but I don't know the immediate steps to take to grow.

NANCY: Well, the immediate step to take to grow is first that you find a job that you think is enough to support yourself and take it.

NETTIE: It's hard to say which comes first, isn't it? If she could do that, she would.

FRAN: That's the cart-before-the-horse kind of thing.

NANCY: It's scary to take those steps, but it's essential to get better because no one's going to do it for you.

FRAN: When I work, I look right, act right, and I do a great job but—I don't feel anything. I'm numbed by the entire situation and I feel nothing. By just being here, you know, in our group—I just looked around and saw a lot of people in that same pain.

LOTTIE: It doesn't let up, the pain.

ANDREA: It's self-inflicted.

LOTTIE: It's as though there's this haze over your head and you can't seem to get on with your life.

GENINE: We talked this morning about recovery or recovering being a process, and all the things I used to not do because I was too busy binging and vomiting. I find that the behavior still persists, but less frequently, and I feel great. I'm happy with myself. I accept the fact that this happens, how often it happens. But when I look at the past where I was binging and vomiting five times a day and that was all I could do and I stayed in the house for two years, there's a big difference! I have a good job; I go out; I have friends. Yet, you know, I want to speed it up. When am I going to recover? When is going to be the day I'm going to say "recovered?" I never heard of a recovered bulimic, and some day I'd like to say I'm *recovering* and that's okay.

I wanted to say one other thing about values. I've learned a long time ago that at some point I can't tell the difference between what I want and what my parents want, what's the projection that I think they want me to have. And my therapist once said to me, "Genine, you don't even know what you want because you're either defying them or trying to get their approval." And it's true. Sometimes what it comes to a decision, say about getting married, I either *not* want to get married to defy them, or *get* married for their approval, but *it's them! What do they want! Not what do I want. I don't know what I want.*

SALLY: When you talk about recovery—I've been an anorexic for about three years now and I've never thrown up and I never take laxatives; I just didn't eat. But I know for three years I didn't like being it and I was waiting for that day when a Messiah would come and the next day I'd wake up and, "Hey, I'm cured; I'm back to normal, back to everything." But I took a look one day and I said, "I'm waiting, I'm waiting. I'll be here in a wheelchair at seventy and I'll still be waiting." I just decided on my own—I didn't fall back on the defense mechanisms that I was using—I mean, I was working nine hours a day and going to school to get my mind on other things, you know, and I was using this as an excuse, "Oh, I can't eat, I'm too busy working." I just said, "Drop all this, the defense mechanisms. It's all a game I'm playing." And I just took it on myself and I said I'm going to do it, you know, I'm going to put on weight. I'm not going to do it for other people who look at me and say, "put some meat on your bones." I'm going to do it for myself.

Physically I've only gained six, seven pounds, which is not much, but mentally, in knowledge, I think I've gained a lot of weight just by doing that and just by looking back at the dumb things I used to do, the dumb defense mechanisms I used in order to make up for the way I was eating or, so to say, not eating. Now I look at it and in knowledge I've really gained a lot. *I think that recovery is really mental before physical.* I mean, so far, I've changed in the past year very much, mentally, even though physically it may only be six pounds. People look at me and tell me I've really changed; they tell me I look a lot better.

NANCY: I think that's really a good point, because I think recovering doesn't mean how much you're eating or throwing up. *Recovering means how are you behaving differently, how you're doing things differently, and how you feel differently.* Another thing we are talking about is happiness and peace and doing things that make you feel good. You don't know what makes you feel good because you're always eating and throwing up.

A real important thing for me to get better was to find a little thing that made me feel better and to do that when I could and to accept it. It was, for instance, like taking a bath. That was like something that really made me feel good. So the few times when I was eating and binging all the time, if I could just take a bath for five minutes and it gave me that little bit of peace or happiness, it was worth it. Each of you have to find that, whatever it is, some little thing, and it gets to get bigger and bigger because you get to be able to do more and more.

LUCY: That's what I like doing; it gets me to work in the morning. I take a bath and I feel peace.

GENINE: When you mentioned recovery, I wanted to say—I've never eaten and thrived as much as I have now, but I think part of it is because I know a lot of things that I used to do were unhealthy. I didn't feel good about them. I don't do those things anymore. I have more time right now. I'm not sure what to do with more time. I'm trying to fill it up. I don't think I'm progressing. I'm just getting on, finding more little things that give me pleasure rather than big things, like picking a career right now.

NETTIE: But would you say your awareness now is a stage further than you were?

GENINE: Oh, yes.

NETTIE: How long have you been ill?

GENINE: I've been ill about ten years.

SALLY: When you speak of free time, I know that there used to be free time for me, but the free time used to have to be labor or some kind of manual work where I'd be burning up calories. There was an obsession to burn up the food that I put in, but now I know when it comes to free time I could just sit down. I could do something pleasurable, like drawing, something that really gives me pleasure in my free time that's not burning up whatever I put in. That was really one big step, also, to be able to sit down after eating and not have to go jog forty miles or something like that.

Or another pleasure was just being able to eat the things that I like and not just using my willpower, like looking at a piece of cake and having your mouth water, but knowing you're strong enough to deny yourself of it. Now, I can actually sit down and eat the cake and not be the strong person—not—I'm not saying I'm not strong, but not just being the person that was depriving herself of everything she liked. Now it's like letting pleasure into your life. That was one of the key changes; *allowing pleasure to come into your life.*

LUCY: About a year ago, my hair was starting to get long and I started setting it with the electric rollers, you know. One morning I lifted up my hair to put a piece of hair in the roller and underneath a patch of hair was gone—just like that—one morning. Well, I was devastated. I called my mother and said, "Take me to the hospital, I have cancer, my hair's falling out." But, of course, they diagnosed it that it was alopecia areata, which came from depression and the throwing up and the loss of this and that and everything. My prescription was—well, first they gave me tranquilizers, which I stopped taking right away because I didn't like that. It slows down your body and you get fat.

I was told to get out with people, friends, do things. So, I started. As a matter of fact, I went on a vacation with a girlfriend and then after that, when I came back, anybody that wanted to go out, Lucy would go—to the bars and to the casinos, all over—I'm down in the bay area. We were going out all the time. I was having fun. What I'm trying to find out is that I don't know why I stopped, except that I did replace the compulsion with eating, with drinking.

PAT: The same thing happened to me.

LUCY: I didn't become an alcoholic, but I probably could have. I would get drunk. If the girls all would go out, I would have to drink seven scotch and waters at night and be totally drunk, you know, to think I was having a good time. But I would really get drunk. I even took home my first two strangers at that time; never did that before in my life, and then I hated myself. Then I stopped going out with the girls, stopped that; so now I'm eating again.

NANCY: So you question why you stopped?

LUCY: Yes, I don't know.

NANCY: But you do know. Why?

LUCY: Oh, because it wasn't fun? That was lousy, too.

NANCY: Because it wasn't fun and because of what else?

LUCY: Because I hated myself?

NANCY: Yes.

LUCY: Yes, I didn't like me doing that.

NANCY: You made a choice.

LUCY: So I went back to eating, because I wasn't doing it.

NANCY: But this life-style didn't fit you.

LUCY: Yeah, I know; it wasn't for me.

NANCY: So you do know why.

LUCY: Yeah, I guess. I didn't think of that before.

LOTTIE: But eating or drinking is the same thing; it's both running away.

TINA: You know what strikes me is that we're always so extreme in everything. Everything we do is so extreme. You know, just like when she was talking about she wanted to try to start doing something. You just didn't start a little bit, joining a club, or, you know, doing a little bit here and a little bit there. You went right out and tried to become God knows what, the star of the Bay town scene. Myself, I never do things on a moderate scale. I call it half-assed, because that's really the way I look at it. That's the way my values are. I have to be, like wild, or I do nothing. I do everything in extremes.

I was a drug addict and an anorexic. I'm now bulimic, a former drug addict. I got high and was anorexic at the same time for many, many years, since I was about seventeen, eighteen years old. I've been in a drug rehab program the past two and a half years. Now, when I went in I stopped using drugs, but I still threw up. I threw up for two years—in a therapeutic situation, which was like—If anybody knows anything about the program, it was unbelievable that I could hang on that long doing it, since the group is all about confrontation.

In our group we were talking about confronting our feelings. When you feel something, say something about it. That's pretty much what therapeutics is all about, you know, constantly groups, constantly confrontation. It was very difficult for me in that situation to hold on to the throwing up, but I did. I'm very strong, but I had no friends. I constantly felt like a sneak. I never felt that it was a big deal to give up getting high because *I always felt like the bulimia was worse.* I didn't think that my drug addiction was so bad, because I looked at the bulimia as much more horrible than being a drug addict, much worse and, you know, in that kind of a situation everybody is drug-free and I felt as though I was so much worse than everybody else. I just felt terrible and they knew about it. But I used them, because they didn't know how to handle it, and they thought "Oh, she's sick. It's an illness, a physical illness," and I played along with that.

Then, finally, I came down to New York and I was faced again with living in the city, with deciding what to do with my life; with having to get a job, which is required; having to save my money; having to move out; and having to select a career role. I graduated from college with Spanish as a secondary, but I never did anything with it, and I was petrified. I wanted to be an actress my whole life, but with the extremes. If I couldn't be on Broadway, I wouldn't even touch it. I never did it. Always blamed it on other things. My father wanted me to be a teacher and that's why I did it, but I never used it.

Some times you have to take things in little steps. I would love to go out and get involved in the theater. But being too afraid to do that, I did nothing. So for me, I had to take a compromise and do something just to get into doing something about my certification. I got my certification; I got a job teaching. I start next week with the emotionally handicapped. I'm going to graduate school. I don't want to be a teacher the rest of my life, but they're like little accomplishments. I have my own place.

I'm so very hard on myself. I think we all are. We all have these stunning goals and, if we don't get them right away, we might get very depressed and give up. I feel that way myself. I don't like making compromises, but I'll tell you something, I—the people that I meet now—before, I used to throw in everybody's face, "I was a drug addict. I was a bulimic," and I'd throw everything right at them. So I had a way to make them feel more compassionate towards me, so that maybe they'd be a little bit more easy on me. I don't do that anymore and *people like me anyway*. People that I meet like me and sometimes that's like a new thing. I always had a gimmick before. I was always manipulative. Not everybody's going to like you, and I've come to accept that too, but it's very hard. I still want to throw up. Sometimes I still want to get high, but I'll tell you something. Doing nothing is just as bad as—or worse—than continuing very destructive behavior. Doing nothing is horrible.

When I lost my job, I was out of work for two weeks. I could barely hold my head up. I was so ashamed. I was just devastated. So I went out and bought myself a suit, a very straight corporate business suit. Then I got my hair cut. I had just moved into my own apartment. I said to myself, "Fix the apartment and keep going to the interviews." It's very hard sometimes to just continue to do things. I don't do everything I should either. But I'm trying—I've come a long way. When I see these little girls, the very, very thin girls, the anorexics, I think I was just like that. A lot of girls that come here never believe that it can be any different. There was a girl in our group that said, "I can't imagine that I could ever not throw up for three or four days." That's why this group is so important.

NETTIE: You said bulimia was even worse than getting high; you felt worse about it.

MAGGIE: I've thought about that. I used to think why can't I be an alcoholic? I've tried all kinds of drugs—well, I've never stuck a needle in my arm. Other than that I've tried everything and hung out where it was easily accessible, and I think I could become an alcoholic. However,

I think I would still have this. I'm bulimic—it's the worst—I guess it's because it's less talked about. There's lots of places for self-help for drugs and alcohol. Everybody knows about drug addiction. Everybody knows about alcoholism.

NANCY: What do you think the difference is though?

LOTTIE: If you're an alcoholic, you can learn to live without taking a drink. *BUT YOU HAVE TO EAT*. You have to change your behavior to accommodate it. I started out being anorexic and bulimic. I'd go through eating, then starving, and try all kinds of diets. I'm not like that anymore. I don't own a scale. I don't get on a scale, even though when I came here today and as I went down the stairs I saw the scale, took my shoes off, hopped on. My mother said, "You're sick." I said, "I know; that's why I'm here." But I still weighed myself. We have to learn to eat.

TINA: I have to learn to live with the societal images on the cover of every magazine that tells me how I should look, feel, smell, and dress. Also, eating is a part of everything. They say to you, the first thing, "Where do you want to go to eat?"

LOTTIE: That doesn't bother me. I can't eat by myself. I live by myself and I know what to buy. I know what's nutritional. We all know about that more, probably, than anyone else. We know the calories, too. But yet, when it comes to bringing the food home to my house, I can't sit down—maybe I'm lazy—I can't sit down and make myself a meal. I could do it for about a week, but then I just freak out. I go back and forth, from food in the refrigerator to nothing in the refrigerator. I can't tell you how many thousands of dollars I've gone through already on food. I can't feel comfortable with food in my refrigerator. I can go out to eat. I went out to eat last night with my boyfriend. I ate fine. It didn't bother me at all. I even drank a few drinks at dinner. I was fine.

NANCY: How were you feeling yesterday?

LOTTIE: Before I went? I wasn't going to go, because I had binged after work and I felt guilty and my head hurt and I just felt terrible. My boyfriend knows about this, and he just said, "Come on, Lottie, just go. It doesn't matter how you feel or what you look like; just go. Maybe it'll make you feel better." I did and at first I felt, "I don't want to be here." There were people I didn't know. I didn't feel like socializing and I'm normally a pretty sociable person. Then it lifted. I started getting into the conversation with these people and I started to enjoy myself and the food did not bother me. I ate, and that was it. I went to the bathroom, and I went to the bathroom. That's *all* I did.

NANCY: Did you feel more in control than you do at other times? Did you feel more in control of yourself? An important part for me about getting better was to start distinguishing how you felt last night differently than how you feel other times.
LOTTIE: I felt terrible when I left work.
NANCY: But you fought it.
LOTTIE: No, I didn't. I ate a whole cheesecake after work.
NANCY: But you didn't stay home.
LOTTIE: Right, I didn't stay home.
SALLY: That's a step forward, I would think.
LOTTIE: I was going through a phase a few months ago where I was forcing myself to go out, forcing myself to call my friends. I would go out with my girlfriend and her husband. You think you don't do threesomes, but you do and you can. I would do that and really enjoy myself. But then what happens is that maybe I'll slip and I'll binge and I'll feel guilty and that guilt keeps me home. If only I could fight my way out of that guilt and say, "So, what the hell. You look like hell, you feel like hell, but just go. If these people can't handle you for what you are right now, then find other people that can." Like Tina was saying, we're so extreme. My normal schedule is going to college two nights a week; going to work every day during the day; going to the ballet whenever I can fit it in, two nights a week, and that's the whole week. I mean, when do you have time to breathe? When do you even have time to think of how you feel? You're too busy running, running and running and running.
SALLY: It's a vicious cycle that you get caught up in. I know, I was doing it. I was going to school five days a week, eight to eleven-fifty, working twelve to nine waitressing, and then teaching dance, too, sometimes after that. Weekends, I'm with a professional dance team, too, so my weekends were either training with the dance team or performing shows. So I was on a vicious cycle, and when it came to eating, I didn't have time to eat. I'd say, "I can't eat, I've got to go to work. I can't eat, I've got to go teach dance."
LOTTIE: I go to Elaine Powers and work out during lunch and then go to ballet at night.
SALLY: Mentally you're burning yourself out. Besides, physically I was burning out my body. I was walking around like a zombie, doing what I had to do. That was it. When it came to leisure time, I would say, "No you can't do any leisure; you're too busy."
TINA: But that part of the symptom sometimes has nothing to do with

recovery. You can be throwing up all the time and still be *recovering* because you're involved in other activities. Or you can have stopped throwing up, but be doing everything else and running away from your problems. Maybe recovery is being able to sometimes, at some point, stay alone with one's self and enjoy yourself.

NANCY: You have to like yourself.

LOTTIE: Be easy on yourself. We're all so hard on ourselves.

ANDREA: I found the hard way that the symptoms get a lot worse in the beginning of therapy. And I can remember four years ago when I started to throw up. I vomited maybe once a day and then it got to a point where it was three times a day, you know, before breakfast, at lunchtime, then I would go home and vomit, and bitch all afternoon. I have a stressful job, like yours, Lottie. I've got one of those jobs in which I've got to keep up with everything. And I do, but it's just that some days I say to myself, "What the hell am I going to get out of this?"

I'm pushing all the time; I'm running six miles everyday. I keep my food intake going. I'm not anorexic, but I'm bulimic. I don't have time for leisure. For instance, if I eat something, I say I don't want to vomit so I'll just eat a little and I'll spend the whole night fighting that. I'll spend the whole night, until ten or eleven o'clock, running or exercising and not go out. I did that for a long time. I never went out. And then I said, what am I doing? It's always either/or! The thing we're all realizing now is it's either/or. *There is an in between,* and I have to distinguish what else is more important to me. What would really benefit myself, instead of the running, the thinking about the food, the obsession with the calories. For one thing, running takes so much time!

FRAN: I used to spend a lot of time working out, meaning, when I got up in the morning I did yoga. As I brushed my teeth I did my exercises. Even in the car with the red light, I did my exercises. I was compulsive with everything I did. And it was real important that I looked exactly right. I don't do all that anymore. I don't compulsively work out or take dance classes because I didn't really know if I enjoyed it. I was doing it just so I could be thin, stay thin, and burn up all my calories.

I'm at the point now where I don't know what I like at all. All the things I thought I liked, I'm not sure about now. I skied all my life because it made my dad real happy. He loved it that his little daughter went skiing. So I used to ski. I hated it. I always thought I was going to die. I hated it. I spent my life doing things that everybody was so happy with me for doing. Then I said, "What about me?" and I stopped doing them, and no one's happy with me anymore. Not that they're not happy with me, it's just that I was going to be *the one.* I was bright, I was attractive, and I was just going to conquer the world and that was part of what kept me going. Then, when I realized I was doing all this but I wasn't being happy, I told my parents. My family said, "No one ever asked you to be that or do that. We don't really care." That flipped me right out.

PAT: I'm Lottie's mother. She was always so concerned with what we thought or what we wanted! If all of you girls could just realize that all we really want is your happiness! It's not your *perfect* job or your *perfect* education that we want for you. We want that you're happy—happy with life and with yourselves. That's all we want.

GENINE: I think that's true, that all a parent really wants is for their children to be happy. But then, I think they have ideas on what happiness is, what it is to them. It's things, maybe, that they didn't have or they didn't achieve. A mother who never went to college may want her child to make it, especially if she's bright. I was the bright one, and my parents had all these ideas for me. I kind of got lost and I didn't know what I myself wanted, because I was so busy trying to please them, wanting to hear my dad say, "I'm proud of you." But then I think—it's like when men look at me or anybody tries to get close to me, I think if they only knew what I was really like. Sure, I appear nice and I'm bright and I've got my MBA and I'm this and I'm that, but if they only knew what I was really like they wouldn't like me, and it makes me angry. When people look at me, it makes me really angry, hostile.

NANCY: Why are you crying, Lucy?

LUCY: Because I feel that way, too. If they only knew. I always say that if a guy really got close to me, he probably wouldn't like me anyway because I'm not nice. I haven't been nice, and since I eat so crazy, I'm miserable. My sister is a couple of years older than I and the two of us are best friends, or were. I've totally destroyed it. She's very much the opposite of me, in that she can sit and eat like a normal person. She and I worked for the same firm about two years ago. She was separated. We each had our own home around the block from each other and so we were together all the time, eating together and whatever. When she and I would eat together, I was like an animal eating and she just ate normal. She still does and I'm like this.

MELINDA: Because you're possessed by eating. That's the whole thing.

LUCY: And when I sit down with her, she'll say to me, "Lucy, relax," and I say, "I can't." And then I just eat everything in sight. Inside I'm so tight and crazy! And now she just had a baby. She calls me and I talk to her, but I'm miserable. I'm the godmother and I haven't seen the baby in two weeks. She'll call me at work. "How are you doing today, Lucy?" And I say, "How do you think I'm doing?" I guess I'm asking her for sympathy. Or I say, "Leave me alone. I don't feel good. I don't want to talk to you. I don't want to see you."

GENINE: When my sister had a baby a few years ago, I went through a whole bunch of feelings, like jealousy, and then I couldn't own up to it. I felt, how can I resent my sister having a baby? What a rotten person I am. I hate this baby. I love this baby. I have ambivalent feelings. I know what it's like. You eat and you eat not to feel, so as not to acknowledge that you're a human being and you're allowed to have and love at the same time; and you're allowed to be jealous of your sister and that it won't kill her even though your fantasy is that you will eat her up and kill her.

LUCY: Can you imagine, I even looked at her, and thought, she's ten pounds heavier than I am now and she just had a baby. Shit, she's actually going to lose that and she's going to be thinner than I am, too, on top of all this. That's sick.

GENINE: And if you were to sit down with her, she'd probably say the same thing about you. Look at you, you're this, you're that, look how wonderful you are, your career . . .

LUCY: When she says things like that, or when people say, "Hey, you got it all," I say, "I don't want to hear that. I don't want to hear that. Why don't you say something to me like 'I can understand how you might be lonely.' " But she doesn't say that. Instead, she's so happy.

GENINE: That you could kill her.

SALLY: You're not expressing yourself to her either. That's really the key thing, to express yourself. There's such a block in expression. Me and my mom went through fighting matches. We used to fight constantly. We'd sit down at dinner and she would say, "Why don't you eat?" "I'm not hungry." Then there would be "Eat this, eat that," and I'd say, "No, I'm not hungry."

But then there was a time, I think it was already World War III or World War IV that we had gone through at this point, and we were screaming. We had it out really good. My dad was putting earplugs in his ears because we were going at it so. I ran in my room again and slammed the door. I know when I fight things come out that I don't want to say. I just get so hostile that a lot of the wrong things come out. Anyway, this time I took out a pad and instead of writing in my diary I wrote out a long, long note. I folded it up and I was going to throw it out, but then I decided to give it to my mom. I said, what the heck. I went into the room and I handed it to her and I ran out. I made sure I wasn't in the room when she read it.

In this note was all my feelings. She came into my room afterwards and we just sat down and we talked. This time it was from the heart. It wasn't from, like, the devil or anything, and since then we've been writing to each other a lot. I find sometimes when you talk to somebody something's going to come out that you don't want to say or the wrong thing'll come out. When you sit down and talk to somebody not everything comes out that you want to come out. It's not always easy to express, looking into the person's eyes, especially since you know that by being anorexic you're hurting this person and by talking to them sometimes you feel the hurt inside of you and you can't say it. So I find that by writing notes, it's such an outlet. We've been doing it for, I'd say, seven months already, and I've made such progress it's unreal. It's just helped us so much. You could just say anything in a letter and when they read it, just make sure you're not in the room.

MELINDA: All of the things that have come out, I think, has helped both of us, not only her and not only me, but *both* of us. It's been a tremendous communication. Although we thought we were so close and we could speak about anything, drugs, alcohol, fellows, whatever you want, or we'd go to a disco and really rap for hours—there was still a block. There were certain things we could not communicate about. No matter what, it meant a fight. When it came to food, it meant screaming and hollering and throwing and kicking, where nobody wound up having dinner because we all got so upset about what was going on. These letters really have made me understand a lot more.. I think it made Sally open up a lot more. There were things that I wouldn't say to her, but yet when I was answering the letter, I could express a lot more or say a lot of things that I wouldn't or just never said.

SALLY: And do it any time. That was the great thing. I'd be in school, at a lecture about math or anything like that, and I'd just start thinking to myself about something. I'd decide to write about it. The letter could take me three days to write because when I just feel something, I write it down to her, just to express it. Sometimes, out of nowhere, you'll just have a thought. It could depress you, the thought of something, but if you just write it down, it helps a lot, too. And then to hand it to somebody is like the biggest thing. You get a reply or feedback from it. That really helps. The biggest thing is really to let out your feelings. Penting up inside, you just get ulcers and eat yourself away.

LUCY: It's easier to tell my sister—I haven't thought about this for a while—"I love you, but I also hate you." Or that, "I love the baby, but I also hate her." I'm always focusing on these bad things about me, so sometimes I can't see the good and sometimes I can't say to my sister, "I love you," because all I can focus on is the jealousy.

I don't know if I said this already, but I did tell her that I was very jealous, and the greatest gift in my life was that on my twenty-something birthday my sister apologized to me for being so rotten to me as a kid. I thought, isn't that nice that somebody would acknowledge it, because she said she was a kid and she didn't have any understanding. She was jealous, she was jealous of *me*.

FRAN: There's something that I wanted to bring out. I send letters to my parents, and I wish my mom was here—she's downstairs in the group session—which is to me, a gift. A gift that she cares enough to come so far as to come here and sit in that meeting and that she knows there's a problem and she loves me. I know that now. I never thought she did. I used to write letters and I never got responses. When I was growing up, I never thought I was real, that I existed.

Once my parents, as a present, got me a carpet. It had been secondhand, and when it rained it used to smell like it was chemically cleaned and an odor used to come whenever it rained and it got damp. I'll never forget that I said, "You know, this carpet really smells." And my mother said, "No, it doesn't." Well, damn, if every time that carpet stank, I didn't smack myself and say, "It doesn't smell." That just sums up—sums up the fact that the reality was my mother's. All I wanted her to think was "You exist as you," but I was so busy existing for feedback, any kind of feedback! Tell me I'm right, tell me I'm wrong, just tell me! I need someone to tell me because I don't exist if you don't tell me I do. I wanted to share this, because it's always in my mind. The carpet, the green carpet that STANK, IT DID STINK, because it smelled to me and *I know* the carpet smells! But now *I know* my mom loves me and she came here to the family member meeting. She may never have written me back, but she got the letters, and I wrote them.

NANCY: And that helped you, too, that your feelings were being expressed. Didn't it feel good just to know that you could let it out?

FRAN: Yes, that felt good, but I needed more. I might never get a reply back from her, but I'm learning to accept that the carpet *did* smell. And she's here now.
NANCY: There's a lot of people that haven't spoken. Does anyone want to speak? You're here because you wanted to participate.
BETTY: Getting on to the subject of writing, I did that around three weeks ago. I hadn't talked to my mother for around two months, and I figured, well, this has got to end. So I sat down and wrote the letter, twelve pages by the time I was finished, and I mailed it. It didn't work out too good. She read it. But she's been a very sick woman all of her life, so she lives in a world of twisted reality. She did call me up because my sisters forced her to.

Fran, you're lucky. You feel your mother loves you. I don't feel that and never have. Some people can say, "I know my problems are dealing with who I am." I'm in conflict with my family's value system, so since I've been little, I've been constantly told that I'm evil. That made me think I was evil inside. I've been verbally told since I've been little, that I'm evil. I'm independent. The devil's in me. Last night, the thought of coming here today scared me so I went on a binge. I came here today to try to get some help and, listening to everybody, I don't feel so alone anymore. I always thought it was me.
ANDREA: This happens to me a lot and I told you before that my throwing up got a lot worse when I started therapy, the reason being that you're *facing feelings*. You're used to putting your feelings aside, by drinking, taking drugs, eating, whatever.
BETTY: See, I always blocked pain and I became strong. You fight me, I'll become stronger. The therapist said, "Okay, we've got to relive all the pain." I said, "No, I want to keep it locked up. That's the way I deal with it." Thirty years old, I've never been drunk. I've never used drugs. I don't smoke. And all of a sudden, since he's started bringing the pain out, I don't go to him any longer because he was dwelling, eight months, in the past, and I was getting tired of it. Plus he was $120 a week in fees. I live alone and I take care of myself. I have a very good job, but $120 a week is ridiculous. Then I started binging after I stopped seeing him, but he brought out a lot of emotion. I mean, I felt guilty just saying, "I hate my mother."
NANCY: You have to live with pain to get beyond it.
BETTY: Well, that's what he said.

NANCY: Also, you're probably so rageful now that, you know, your eating and throwing up is like rage.

BETTY: Yeah, it's like I've become very frustrated and I don't have anybody to turn to, so it's self-destructive. That's what it is. I mean, I have to be honest. I have thought of killing myself many times, though I haven't done it. You know, you talk about people getting to know you and not liking you—I always felt, if your own mother can't like you, how can anybody else? If she doesn't like you, who the hell is going to?

NANCY: Well, you said at the beginning that your mother was sick, so you have to understand that she may not be able to.

BETTY: Well, I said since I was little that when she dies I'll be free, but I realize that's not true. My mother wants us to live with guilt. This is even a harder thing to say, but since we've been little she's always said on every holiday, "I'm not going to see this holiday. You kids are killing me." All her misery was our fault. So one day she says, "I'm dying. I want to die." So I went into the kitchen and I took a knife and said, "Here, at least have the guts to do it." She shut up. I said, "Then you don't really want to die, do you, because if you want to die here's your opportunity." So I said, "Shut up. I don't want to hear you anymore." That's a horrible way to talk to your mother.

ANDREA: You were expressing your own emotions.

NETTIE: This brings us back to full circle, doesn't it, because Nancy started talking about taking values into your own system from your parents, and I think in a way you're describing having taken values in that were so destructive to you, that now you're having to reconstruct values that are going to be your own. It is different when you have to accept the fact that maybe your mother isn't going to read the letters.

BETTY: She reads them, but she never understands.

NETTIE: And that's a whole different thing, because not all mothers are able to because of some of their own hardships.

BETTY: She said something to me on the phone that really made me start thinking. I told her, "God, you've never even hugged me. You don't even kiss me or anything." And she said, "I don't see what's so wrong about that. My mother never kissed me." So when I listened to her I said to myself, "Oh boy, she's probably not responsible." She was only reacting the way she was brought up.

GENINE: You said before how can somebody love me if my own mother couldn't love me. Something we were talking about, that comes up in

every group, some of us, when we open up to our mothers, it all works out, they're able to change with us. But your mother and my mother, they are as much victims or whatever of their environment and their past. My mother, also, is never going to be able to give me something of the things that I need, but that doesn't mean you're not lovable if she can't give you the love that you need. She's losing out too.
BETTY: She lost me as a daughter. I told her that. I said, "I'll be there if you need me to do something for you, but you've lost me as a daughter."

Some young women have not spoken at all, but their silence has been an intense participation for them. Feelings have been expressed that have not crystallized in words for them. Later, weeks afterward, one person who had not been able to speak, would write a letter to express her thoughts and feelings.

The leaders end the session, thanking the group members for contributing to someone else's understanding and learning, as well as to their own. There is a quiet moment, then the group dissolves. Each person is separate again and once more takes on her battle alone.

A fortunate circumstance allows a glimpse into Lucy's future, that is, the future that for her she believes began at *this session.* She told us some weeks afterward that she had been free of her bulimic cycle for a number of weeks and that the quality of life had improved for her immeasurably.

Patsy wrote us a few weeks afterwards of her experience as an anorexic and the ways that she has found to slay the dragon of obsession with food.

I spent most of my time, as far back as I can remember—perhaps from about five years old—striving for and dreaming of great achievements and recognition. This was the message that I got from my parents as to what was important in life. No time was spent just talking to me about feelings, nor was there much physical or verbal love expressed towards me. I never had "mother-daughter" or "father-daughter" talks. My personal life was never of any attention to my practically alcoholic father who only criticized me or ignored me or to my mother who often looked to me for help with her problems or to be an ear for hearing how bad people were . . . As a result I grew up not knowing about friends or love . . . I did not seek out friends because no one was to be trusted.

She thinks that she was preoccupied with food as far back as she can remember, five years of age, although she was not aware of it. More consciously she was obsessed with it since her senior year of high school. Being an active athletic child, she could eat large amounts from time to time and not gain weight—was actually quite thin. Gaining, in her high school senior year, was a shock to her. She tried to diet but kept gaining the weight back. By the end of college she was binging and vomiting three or four times a day, losing weight rapidly.

I then stopped . . . almost "cold turkey." I knew it was wrong and since that time—almost five years ago, I have only binged and vomited a few times—the last time, May 1980.

It was a combination of things that worked, but the main one was that I kept so busy I didn't have time to allow the thought of food to enter my mind. Since it was my behavior, in the past, to act and not to think it made it easy.

But I almost fell apart several times by my efforts to keep busy. It cured the anorexia, but almost knocked me out.

Many, in the effort to change, became obsessed with excessive activity. Patsy feels that she is well on the way to recovery from the "manic activity" and the "constant depression" that were present during her entire life.

A combination of things—therapy, self-help, her own determination—has helped her. She writes that she has learned to move more slowly, to cut down on her excessive activities. She has modified her expectations and goals to a more realistic level. She meditates, jogs, exercises, and *rests*. Socializing is important for her; she plans her meals. She *talks "as much as possible."*

I knew I wanted great achievements for myself, but did not realize how physically hard I was pushing myself. I also knew my achievements never really made the depression lift or made me happy. So I tried to get closer to people and found that I don't know the first thing about life, people, love—I also realized that when I talked, the cravings and subconscious stress of accomplishing and responsibilities eased, even though I was very self-conscious and ignorant of how to be a friend after talking and socializing. I began to feel some miniscule emotion—and to see my accomplishments in the right perspective. (Still have a long way to go, but do see the light!) I began to feel less robot-like and empty.

She helped herself by using gum and hard candy throughout the day, then gradually stopped.

. . . it has been excruciating, and I still suffer from strong and somewhat constant cravings. Jogging and exercising also helped tremendously. Even though I played tennis my whole life this helped more because it gave my mind and body a rest from achieving—unlike tennis—(It may sound like I was a great achiever, but I really have only been average because of the unnaturalness of my behavior.)

Patsy feels that she has been

addicted—(the only word I can use to describe it), to eating. I began to see that I needed the action of eating to cause me to move physically or to think (what little thinking I did).

Thoughts of food, she remembers, were always interrupting and dividing her attention. She would shove some food down and then rush into whatever she was supposed to do "slam bang." It was a life-long behavior and now, in retraining herself, she tries to think before she moves.

. . . and it has worked miracles. In combination with other things I am doing, my mind feels free, at times, from thoughts of food and I don't feel so hyper. This is, as concisely as possible, how I see what's happened. I'm feeling better every day and pray the hell is past me.

Patsy continues now to piece out the things she missed, using many ways to help herself—seeking relationships and relatedness. She comes to the self-help groups—and now her mother comes, too, to the family member group. She wants to come.

And so, with spoken and with written words, the restructuring of one's self goes on. Where the definition has not been clear originally, there may well be another chance through the mediating process of the intellect. It is perhaps the "amended text."

These have been some of the experiences of some of the people suffering at various stages from the symptoms of anorexia and bulimia. They are, by no means, all the experiences of all the sufferers. These young women have given excerpts from *their* text, and even *their* sub-text—the depth and breadth of which another may never glimpse.

IT cannot simply be forgotten
the wounds have not yet healed
It's done with you say—
maybe so . . .
the past has not been buried
in its rightful place
So easy to recall
but not able to forget.
In the quiet moments
of the night
I cry out still
and shake with fear—
a climax of terror
Weeping out of sheer frustration
How well
I remember the nightmare
of self-induced pain
I didn't mean for it
to be this way—
I used to say
Fooling myself that
I was strong
but it takes strength to
face reality.
Finally, I admitted my defeat
a frail child was I—
fallen to my knees.
I chose to try
when death was so near, you see—
with the promise that
something was indeed better
than the horrifying cage
I had locked myself in.

ALLYNNORE TOM

7

Our Commentary

Marian's mind grasped at the world "immature," turning it over like a curious pebble found on a beach. It suggested an unripe ear of corn, and other things of a vegetable or fruitlike nature. You were green and then you ripened; became mature. Dresses for the mature figure. In other words, fat.

She looked around the room at all the women there, at the mouths opening and shutting, to talk or to eat . . . They were ripe, some rapidly becoming over-ripe, some already beginning to shrivel; she thought of them as attached to stems at the tops of their heads to an invisible vine, hanging there in various stages of growth and decay . . . in that case, thin elegant Lucy, sitting beside her, was merely at an earlier stage, a springtime green bump or nodule forming beneath the careful golden calyx of her hair.

MARGARET ATWOOD,
The Edible Woman

True prevention requires that their pleasing superperfection is recognized early as a sign of inner misery.

HILDE BRUCH, M.D.

As we, the Book Committee of the American Anorexia/Bulimia Association, reviewed the material contributed for this project, certain themes, observations, and conclusions seemed to emerge. It is these that we offer as our commentary.

A child is born, becomes adult, then dies. Life comes full circle back to nonexistence. It is in the nature of things.

Many of the accounts suggested to us that we were indeed witnesses to, and for some of us participants in, a desperate paradoxical battle on the part of the anorexic to hold back this natural life process, as if to ensure that she remains fixed in time, as then so do the parents. Thus, it would seem that she attempts to protect them from their death, the ultimate separation.

The anorexics appear to experience their very existence as inseparable from that of their parents, the original source of nurture, however imperfect it may have been, or however much they reject that nurture. Going forward may mean the eventual loss of that source. In the growing person's ascendance to maturity, separateness, and selfhood, there will be a gradual descendance of the original provider by psychic separation and, eventually, physically by death. Therefore, we can understand philosophically and symbolically that the anorexic is facing a threat to her very existence, and that she mobilizes her forces to withstand it and to survive. That those forces are in themselves life-threatening and seem regressive deepens the paradox. (For further reading see Palazzoli 1978: ch. 18.) Of course, there are anorexics who are older, who have entered into certain areas of adulthood, but, for reasons of inner or outer stress, renounce or avoid some part of their adulthood. It is as if they seek to return, symbolically, to an earlier time. They act as if they were there, in a time when there was nurturing and security from without, when there was an illusion of nurturing, or when there was still the possibility of being warmed, held, and fed in a way to make one feel good, secure, and, later, brave. The anorexics, as children and would-be children, act as if there were a choice one could actually make in taking the risk to go forward into life.

We think that the anorexic more precisely personifies resistance to time passing than does the bulimic. The person who has developed bulimic behavior has found a way that initially seemed to hold the answer to meeting the body's compelling urgencies without having to take the consequences. It seems as if she has partially acknowledged the inevitability of going onward, but is unable to brave or tolerate the risks without the mediation of a massive feeding in an attempt to quell the fears evoked. While the anorexic has become, in her distorted view, the resolute conqueror of her body, the bulimic is forever giving in and then cleansing herself in expiation.

We wonder at the force of fear that catches the child at the onset of adulthood. All of us, parents, professionals, and sufferers, would like to find one cause, one cure, one means of prevention. It is hard to believe that this condition defies such specificity. But we think that our look at many families and many sufferers correlates with the findings of those theorists who believe that it is a condition caused by multiple factors, both outside and inside the individual. Converging at a particularly vulnerable time for the growing child, these factors are responsible for the development of behavior that is psychically meant to ward off external and internal threats. (For further reading, Schwartz et al. 1982:20–36.)

The components that predispose one child rather than another to become the afflicted member of the family are several and varied. Some may have been present in the family long before the arrival of the particular child, the anorexic-to-be. Some may be present in the constitutional makeup with which the child comes into the world, and some may be activated by our cultural standards, the mores of today as each individual interprets them.

Hardships, as Dr. Atchley pointed out in chapter 2 and as we have heard from families, such as deaths in families, alcoholism, marital conflicts, disappointments, or illnesses of siblings or grandparents, are all stressors. In these difficult times people's capacity to do, to give, and to cope is stretched to the limit or is inconsistent and confused, even absent. Mothers have traditionally been the ones to set the emotional tone and to provide emotional security for the child. Biologically, a mother is the first to give the child a physical place for being and, most often, the first to give the child a sensual, tactile experience of contact after birth. Gradually, as the infant grows, ideally the mother introduces the nature of apartness and separateness to the new human being physically eager for growth.

It is awesome, we think, that so much rests on mother. When Jane senses that her daughter might not want to grow up to face what her mother contends with in her adult life, she may be touching upon an unconceptualized feeling present in a lot of children who reluctantly go into adulthood, especially those who are later beset with eating disorders. We have seen that many anorexics are described as the *sensitive ones* or the ones who *bear the emotions* for the family. They are described as little mothers, especially to their own mothers, in times of stress in the family. During the course of the illness, they seem to have to go back to being little girls again, as if to make up for the time when they were precociously self-sufficient and taking care of someone else.

It strikes us that mothers represent a formidable role model. When they are over-burdened, unsure of themselves, struggling to achieve mastery over household matters, child raising, and work, or a career, their efforts are observed and incorporated in the child's perception of herself and the world. If the mother manages to do a multitude of things and is a competent person, that is also incorporated—sometimes it becomes impossible to live up to the mother. If the burdens are not shared with support from the fathers, then the children become aware of the imbalance. If the fathers themselves are going through crises and overloads, they are unable to respond to the needs of the children or the mothers.

Sometimes it is not clear to a woman, as it was not to Colleen, that she is submerged and losing herself. But it is clear to a child who, as a consequence, feels her own state of being threatened. The child has to shore up the falling framework of her family, her world.

Fathers traditionally have represented the outside world in our society—at least since Victorian times. While this is changing, they still are the bridge to external achievements and self-sufficiency. Their expectations, their comments, their reactions have an extra charge. Not being in touch continually with the daily details and routines that make a household and home function, they are once removed and may be distant or experienced as distant. Added to this, their cultural programming has taught them to remain aloof from some of the emotionality and strife that is a fact of everyday life with growing children. Their conditions of work often require them to be away physically as well. Therefore, their involvement is of a different nature, but equally important, and integral, to the way the mother reacts to the child, to the way the child responds and to their combined and complementary ways of responding.

The nature of closeness and distance between father and daughter seems most delicate. Some fathers respond to their daughters with too much closeness, others with too much austere authoritarianism. The daughter's emergence into womanhood at adolescence often introduces unexpected feelings in the father's usual way of relating to her.

Father is not only the model for a child's later male-female relationships, but is also a special reflection of being-in-the-outside-world that is to be emulated or rejected. Children identify with and want to be like both parents and gradually emerge with their own personalities. Sometimes these different identifications conflict. When a child tries to "fill in" for the unavailable parent, that child is identifying with the parent in pain and is trying to make it better. In addition, there is a dis-identification with the "bad" (absent or unavailable or for some other reason) parent and a feeling of anger. On the other hand, there may be anger toward the "injured" parent, a feeling that "I don't want to be like that"—that is, in the position of being hurt and put-upon, weak and helpless. It seems to us that whether fathers are actually present or not, they are most influential as they affect the interactions of others. There may well be room in current literature for more discussion of daughters' and fathers' relationships. A recent book, *Passionate Attachments: Fathers and Daughters in America Today* by Signe Hammer, is one literary exploration of this subject.

Unfortunately, in efforts at recovery during anorexia and bulimia, which often examine the past in order to deal with the present, the mother's role seems to carry the burden, almost as if the father's role were tangential. In mental health services and psychotherapies for children, his role seems to have been unduly deemphasized. Only with the emergence of family therapy are fathers, as well as mothers, customarily seen in sessions. From the information given by respondents, it seems to us that fathers may still be underserved and underinvolved in therapy plans for the afflicted child. Should this be the case, then mother's burdens are even greater in that she is doing the emotional work for both herself and her partner, thus perpetuating an old disabling pattern. It may be that fathers, if present, do not feel comfortable in "baring their emotions" and refuse to do so. The demands of work may also make the father's participation difficult. For one or all of these reasons, if the father does not participate, the message to the afflicted child is that mother shares in the emotional fixing up and father simply is, and whatever he is is static and unchangeable.

In contrast, the American Anorexia/Bulimia Association's self-help meetings continue to draw many fathers. The simple fact of scheduling the meeting on Saturday may encourage participation. And parents come to the meetings more often during acute phases of the illness, at a time when fathers are extremely upset about their children and severely discommoded by the daily battles over food and activity.

It has been suggested that anorexia nervosa increases at a time when the position of women is undergoing a cultural change (Palazzoli 1978:245, 246). Certainly in our present climate, there have been many advances made in women's rights and opportunities for career and job fulfillment. It is no longer as strong a cultural norm to expect that a little girl will grow up only to marry and to be a "mommy." She is expected to "be something" as well. As mother is affected by the new wave of womanhood, she may unknowingly expect her daughter to achieve and to take advantage of the new opportunities that she herself was denied. The perceptive or sensitive child incorporates this amorphous feeling. In addition, sexual freedom has loosened the strictures of the past, allowing the daughter sexual expression that may be felt as a pressure and that occurs just at a time when other social and intellectual skills have to be acquired. The mounting demands for achievement and fulfillment of expectations may well present a frightening future.

The mothers, who have lived through at least two wars and who have seen mores change radically since they themselves were raised, are perhaps the most profoundly traumatized, even though they cannot consciously formulate the shock of it all. In middle-class circles, to be "just" a housewife and mother, connotes a sluggishness and an old-fashioned stance, whereas a few decades ago it would have been the fulfillment of a worthy and desirable expectation in becoming a woman. The woman of today must now find out how to nurture so that she and others honor it, and so that she does not lose herself. Just as Colleen and others described, the attempt to redefine one's own self may bring about the *wholeness* of another person, one's daughter. The body, as a metaphor, can then be viewed as an assertive instrument for pleasure and communication as well as a receptor for others' needs.

In examining the questionnaires we received, several topics seem to call for further detailed study. While our reports of family income are similar to those in other surveys which have more systematically investigated those levels, designating AN families in the wide and imprecise category of the middle class, we suggest that further study about the significance of this could be helpful in prevention and recovery.

Middle class is a loose term applied at various times to values or income or both. Both are wide-ranging with values formed by religious and ethnic background, region and educational experience. Income level may range from dependence on two or more wage earners, who can provide a barely adequate amount, to affluence, with considerable funds in savings and investments.

Note that our reports represent a group of people, 71 percent of whom have incomes above $25,000. It seems clear that they are, for the most part, comfortably above the poverty level. But about half have less leeway for extras and half of those are quite marginal (see Appendix table 1F). In those parts of America's population where there is real hunger or in the industrially underdeveloped nations, anorexia nervosa is apparently practically non-existent (Garfinkel and Garner 1982:100–121).

We wonder if there isn't something more in social class setting that should be explored by sociologists and social psychologists, in terms of living patterns, community expectations and acceptance, environmental pressures for conformity, the meaning of largesse in food and clothing, and the many choices or alternatives made possible by the economic level of the family.

One example, one variant, might be that though "middle class" in income at present, a couple (one or both) may have come from a childhood in a family of poverty or very limited means, with early years spent in working toward distant goals, earning money for extras or even necessities—food, clothing, or school expenses, including carfare, books, and lunch money. Their entrance into a different and higher income strata may have come after considerable effort and privation. The couple, now parents, raise a child in the midst of many possibilities, many choices. It is partially their goal coming to be reality, that their offspring will not have to bear the hardships they had to endure.

Given this previous experience, it is perhaps harder for a parent to say no, to frustrate a need, to permit growth-producing situations, to encourage self-reliance, when all the earlier striving has been to provide a home that ensures against want.

Another possible point for study related to "middle class" ideas and values is the subtle regulation of desire for acquisition through television. Its constant use may produce confused attitudes about "what I want," "what I must not want," "what I can have," and "what I cannot have" in the growing person's daily life regardless of the age of the child and the strength of his ability to cope.

In this welter of choices and the understandable uncertainty of parents, the growing child may be left to decide for herself which of many possibilities is appropriate and right. We are told that the child is often a harsher parent to herself, under the circumstances, than the real parent would be. Translated into psychosomatic, or mind-body terms, she may either (restrict) starve herself, or give in (indulge) to the other extreme and gorge herself, after which she feels profound remorse and self-hatred.

In the larger arena, we are impressed with the effect of the constant pressure by the media on the need to be thin, conveying significant cultural norms. Looking back one or two generations from the anorexic's world of today brings us to a time of radical social change in gender ideal. As women's attire became simpler, it was "masculinized" in the second half of the nineteenth century by women who sought more comfort and mobility, but who were part of a subculture of social experimentation. Amelia Bloomer's

"Turkish" trousers in the 1850s were acclaimed by Elizabeth Cady Stanton and others in the women's rights movements. As women ventured out of the Victorian home into the work arena, clothing took on a specific meaning, symbolizing a revolution in women's position in society. By the end of the nineteenth century, such characteristics of reform had "entered the vocabulary of 'fashion'." (Ewen 1982:155)

As consumer goods became more and more available because of mass production, manufacturers took advantage of the desires of the public. By 1920 our historians of fashion state that Bullocks department store in Los Angeles was describing six categories of customers:

1. Romantic, slender, youthful
2. Statuesque—tall, remote, blonde
3. Artistic—enigmatic, suggestive of the "foreign"
4. Picturesque—soft outline
5. Modern
6. Conventional—older, stouter, economical

They continue:

> A new way of understanding oneself in relation to society was emerging. Linked to matters of personal decoration, it broke from a past in which *who you were* in society was a matter of social and economic class. The new structure was more superficially defined, and one's classification was ostensibly a matter of choice. Some might choose "romantic," others "artistic." Social identity, according to the schema, was there on the racks to be bought. (Ewen 1982:230)

Not only did the racks of mass-produced clothes invite comparison and assessment of one's body, but the new industry of motion pictures—and finally television—standardized concepts of feminine attractiveness with an impact not felt before. Magazines presented ways in which one could be more beautiful, beautiful like the stars of film and the models used in the magazines. To this day, magazines show clothes for the pencil slim figure and publish article after article about diet. Getting ahead, being successful, meeting the right man and being happy are all equated with being thin.

Here is a sampling of current featured magazine articles bombarding women over only a few weeks:

"How To Be Your Own Diet Doctor"
"The Most Beautiful Bodies in America: Top Beauties Reveal Their Body Slimming Secrets"
"12 Ways to a Sensual Body—A Shape-Up Guide"
"The Waist-Away Bikini Diet—4 Weeks to a Terrific Figure"
"Lose Up To Two Pounds a Week Without Counting Calories"
"How To Stay Thin Forever"
"How To Stretch Fat Thinner"

None of these articles in themselves may be noxious. Paradoxically, these same magazines seem to be in the forefront of publishing helpful articles for those of their readership who are afflicted. They give clear descriptions of the eating disorders and instructive information about treatment and self-help groups and associations. It is the cumulative power, however, of the continuous clamor to be thin and to diet that gives a strong message to women: they truly better "shape up."

We decry this constant barrage of illusory propaganda. We wish we could all be healthy, maintain a reasonable weight, and not worry about living up to media-hyped cultural ideals. We also wish that appearance would not so frequently come to be the measure of the person. However, it is not so simple as it appears. The opposite side of the coin can present severe problems. To pay no attention at all to appearance, to cling to the rationale that extreme obesity is a perfectly acceptable choice, provides no real solution. Respect for one's person, one's appearance, is a part of our armamentarium—our presentation of ourselves to the world. In our particular present society, our plenty and the nature of our lives create the need to regulate our weight ourselves, that is, if we wish to remain healthy and not too far outside the norm for appearance.

Suzie Orbach, in *Fat is a Feminist Issue*, recommends ways in which women can overcome their slavish devotion to cultural standards. Marcia Millman, in *Such a Pretty Face*, points up advantages and gratifications in obesity despite cultural views to the contrary and describes organizations which offer support and fellowship for the different and heavy woman.

The problem is one of feeling that it is imperative to conform to the norm in order to deem oneself worthy, as if one's self were wholly defined by outer manifestations of the body. Tragedy occurs when one's self-love is built on supports too frail to bear the weight of ordinary everyday demands. We can only conclude that this condition, anorexia and bulimia, which seeks an extreme way to control one's fat, may truly be a metaphor for our paradoxical time of plenty in the midst of starving world populations. The anorexic/bulimic herself, because of the convergence of many factors, is the fallout, an incidental consequence of our ways. It may well be that anorexia will be less prevalent in years to come as new and different aspects of our society emerge.

Whatever the underlying sociological causes in the broad picture, the individual family faced with the intense personal crisis of the condition must consider what to do for its own individual needs. An understanding of the culture-wide philosophical implications may be valuable, but in dealing with this life-destroying illness, the family must contend with the here and now and the particular.

This major crisis may be of several years' duration. It is an experience that destroys one's confidence. Previous ways of handling situations are not effective and one's power and influence within the family have changed. *Outside assistance is essential at this time in the form of some kind of psychotherapy as well as appropriate medical care.* It is not so much that one family member or another is to be targeted as the person at fault or the cause of the illness, but rather the family is so involved that one individual cannot see the forest for the trees and therefore needs to allow an outsider—a professional person—to be a more objective part of the family's efforts to resolve the dilemma. It will be hard to let someone else into the family circle and there may be upsetting conversations and disagreements. But these sessions will refocus priorities and needs and will supply a supportive frame for the work to be done. The parents may find themselves encouraged to recall events and incidents in the past. They need not be defensive if they understand that the relationships and happenings of the past are to be used not to place the blame, but to change the present. Taking responsibility for one's relationship to another and asking oneself what should be changed is very different from staying mired in guilt for one's past attitudes or actions. To realize that how one related was not good for the child can produce great sadness and remorse, but after the initial awareness, there needs to be a reconciliation with oneself. Parents may have done the best they could at the time. Looking back can show how it should have been different, but there is no way to redo it. The only way, as several fathers said, is to "face up to it." It seems our nature to say we were bad or we were good. There are, of course, unfortunate exceptions, but for most of us our fallibility as parents defies absolutes. We were both good and bad.

Some parents quote one of the tenets of Alcoholics Anonymous or Al-Anon, "Detach with love." It is a helpful concept. Mothers have to learn with each trivial detail of everyday what that means. There must be an effort to be objective, to realize that recovery is slow, that there are many setbacks. Above all, it must be remembered that the victim needs to learn how to be in charge of herself—in a benevolent, constructive way.

There is no blueprint for handling special foods, eating habits, temper tantrums, manipulativeness, and vomiting episodes. The general rule of thumb is that coercion won't help and is ill-advised. The victim's request for help with regulation should be honored if it is to be a truly mutual effort, not simply "mommy or daddy" taking over. If the situation becomes one where parental authority is used to try to make the anorexic eat, it will usually amount to little more than a power struggle. Parents have many commitments and many responsibilities toward themselves and other children in the family. Excessive focus on the victim throws other relationships out of whack. It will be helpful in the long run to concentrate on some of those relationships. The victim, though self-centered in her illness, is quite aware of and upset about the sadness and confusion she is causing. She needs all the help she can get in not feeling she is the sole center of the universe. A mother who allows herself, at an appropriate time, an afternoon of going to a museum, shopping, or visiting with friends, shows her daughter that separateness is a part of life—that one can love without the need to be together all the time. "Love and let go" or "detach with love" are deceptively simple phrases, but are profound in their respect for helping individuals grow to be autonomous.

It is unfortunately true that not all victims of anorexia recover in the full sense of the word. For some sufferers and their families there may be no happy ending in sight. The wear and tear of chronicity is diminished somewhat by finding support groups as well as mental health guidance through local community mental health centers and clinics. It is equally important to find ways to live around the chronic illness, without all activity and attention focussed on the sufferer.

As Dr. Atchley has pointed out, there are many different ways of treating these eating disorders. There is no one proven way that will be effective for everyone, but many courses of treatment that can turn out well. We do see psychotherapy of some kind as important for every sufferer and family—and it would appear that our participating families agree—for help in dealing with the illness and aiding in recovery. We sum up some of the salient issues brought up in sessions and in questionnaires for both patient and therapist.

1. The psychotherapist should be knowledgeable about the illness, its treatment, and the medical implications of self-starvation, binging, and purging. Families can assist their therapists by acquainting them with the literature they have come across.
2. The therapist must be well-trained in one of the mental health disciplines of which psychotherapy is a part.
3. There must be a good working relationship between the patient and therapist. There must, in other words, be a "spark," a good feeling about the encounter, that can develop into trust. Caution: This does not mean that you will always love or agree with the therapist.
4. Families should think of themselves as potential contributors to their

family member's returning health, rather than as the cause of the illness.

5. There will be times when the sufferers will not want any other people in their therapy or talking with their therapist. This should not be taken as an offense. For older children in particular, it is necessary that they have this distance in which to practice privacy and autonomy. Parents and family members may want to have another therapist for themselves, one recommended by the primary therapist.
6. Stay with therapy through rough spots and, if you have a disagreement with the therapist, talk about it with the therapist. If eventually you are not comfortable, ask for a consultation with another professional. And finally, after you have given a lot of consideration to it, if you really can't work with this person, do not feel you have to stay, but *do* find someone else.
7. Your child's (wife's, husband's) therapist will speak with you from time to time. Contents of their sessions, however, will not be divulged.
8. An older adolescent or older adult may not require as much contact between parents (family members) and therapists, except where extreme dependency or illness requires parental care.
9. There must be continual medical care and surveillance in conjunction with psychotherapy. Where there is purging by vomiting, dental care will also be required.

Psychotherapists would do well to understand that families need to be educated in the process of psychotherapy, in how one becomes a patient. One must be helped to "trust" the process just as one is helped to "trust" the therapist. Therapists, apparently, sometimes do not clue in the parents, leaving them with a feeling of being excluded and undesirable. Their baffled and angry reaction is destructive to mutual efforts and may well inhibit recovery.

The alertness and awareness required to recognize AN is no doubt increasing. However, the important role of the physician—pediatrician, gynecologist, or internist—in ascertaining the diagnosis and in recommending and participating in treatment can still be improved. As we learned from the contributing families, had some practitioners been more aware of the possibility of an eating disorder, the diagnosis could have been made more quickly and treatment started earlier. We hope for more continuing education courses, conferences, and literature to alert the medical practitioner to preventive, diagnostic, and treatment possibilities in AN. Given wider professional exposure to the anorexic and bulimic syndrome, the pediatrician may then listen with greater sensitivity as a young girl bemoans her weight even though she is thin, or as a mother worries about her child's diet even though it may sound as though the mother is "overconcerned." The gynecologist has an opportunity to pick up sounds and signs of distress, especially when there is a symptom as marked as disturbances in the menstrual cycle. Bulimic behavior, particularly, is so hidden that physicians will not detect it unless they know about the symptoms.

At present the availability of treatment is far greater than at any other time. The quality of treatment has improved with the increase of the syndrome of AN/Bu. As Dr. Atchley has pointed out, the disorders are treated with many approaches and in many different settings. In-hospital and out-patient treatment will be used as required. A variety of drugs will be prescribed, which may be directed at the disorder itself or emotional and physical conditions related to or existing with the AN/Bu. Medical and psychological specialists combine their efforts to mend both body and mind. Group, individual, and family therapy will be employed according to the cooperative decisions of the patient, her immediate family members (if appropriate), and those who are planning treatment.

For the most part care of the patient is obtained through one private practitioner who calls upon associates when consultation or special therapy is needed. Efficient and convenient treatment is sometimes found in a medical-psychiatric center, a community mental health clinic, or a hospital with an out-patient unit in which the several aspects of treatment can be coordinated. Unfortunately, too few of these facilities are available or prepared to treat eating disorders. With in-service training to accustom personnel to the nature and treatment of anorexia and bulimia, existing mental health centers can establish units, especially if the need is brought to the attention of the administration. These centers, in liaison with hospitals, can provide continuity of care. Recently a few such units have been developed, due to the initiative of concerned professionals or members of our association.

It is imperative that the overall cost of care be reduced for the members of families and single people (especially the older sufferer) who simply cannot survive financially under the catastrophic weight of such a long-term illness. A mental health center or clinic is in a position to have a sliding fee scale for the psychotherapy, which is usually not fully covered by insurance. The combined efforts of families and the American Anorexia/Bulimic Association may bring about urgently needed change in the limited hospital coverage of some insurance companies. We wish to emphasize that practitioners, both medical and psychological, are available, but they need to learn more about AN/Bu. Associations, such as ours, made up of professionals and sufferers and their families extend and encourage educational services for other professionals in continuing education, seminars, and conferences.

School personnel have become more alert to the child who may be becoming anorexic. It is our hope that teachers, guidance counselors and other counseling personnel, school nurses and sports coaches will keep in mind the conditions under which anorexia/bulimia seems to flourish, namely, competitive arenas where expectations sometimes can become translated into excessive efforts that require more than the growing body can give. It is unfortunate that we hear of the too eager athletic or gymnastics coach or ballet instructor who encourages excessive dieting and purging behavior. This may be where the potential anorexia/bulimia finds fertile soil for developing. There is a narrow, fine, but definite, line between being fit and pushing one's body to unnatural limits. School can be the setting in which conformity of shape and weight can be addressed in seminars and classes in physical and health education. In-service training and orientation toward restructuring the views of school personnel may be an initial step in such a preventive program.

In recent times there has been an increased interest in running, jogging, and other forms of imaginative exercise, including dance, aerobics, and gymnastics. This reflects, in part, a new and healthy respect for the care of the body. Strenuous exercise seems to provide a kind of natural high, the product of the endorphins discussed by Dr. Atchley. These hormones give us a feeling of exhilaration and well being. Originally, in man's early development, these endorphins flooding the body in physical exertion and even in the early stages of starvation, were an important survival mechanism. Researchers, among them Dr. Hans Huebner, hypothesize that these complex hormones are released at a certain point in the anorexic and bulimic starvation process, as well as in exercising, producing a euphoria that is hard to give up, thus making the anorexic/bulimic behavioral syndrome appear to have similarities to an addictive-like state (Huebner 1981). An exploration of the mechanism brought into play in the various Eastern religions which involve fasting might be productive in helping us understand the tenacity of these behaviors. Other researchers (for example, Wurtman et al. 1981:2–15) at the Massachusetts Institute of Technology are exploring the physiological mechanisms having to do with carbohydrate cravings and possible chemical ways of suppression in excessive over-eaters.

The work of psychoanalytic inquiry and research has enriched professional and nonprofessional understanding of intrapsychic factors. We think, of course, of Dr. Hilde Bruche in the United States and Professor Arthur Crisp in England, who have made major contributions to theory and technique of treatment. It is also in the years of intensive study of individual psychodynamics and psychosomatic processes, such as the study group of analysts of twenty years' standing under the auspices of the Psychoanalytic Association of New York that knowledge has increased. Drs. C. Philip Wilson, Charles Hogan, and Ira Mintz, editors of *The Fear of Being Fat: The Treatment of Anorexia Nervosa and Bulimia*, and others who have been a part of that group, classify anorexia as a psychosomatic illness (Wilson 1983:2). Dr. Wilson describes the process as monumental attempts (of the ego) to defend against the fear of being fat, a fear on which "conflicts from every level of development—pre-oedipal, oedipal, adolescent, and adult—are displaced and masked by the fear" (Wilson 1982:233, 1983:9).

It is in the above areas that we are impressed with the urgent need to proceed with more research. While it is not within our scope or power to provide money, the number of associations across the country could join together to support, encourage, and even help to legislate such research by lobbying efforts.

A recent increase in special groups for the persons presently affected predominantly by bulimia are developing. As Dr. Atchley mentioned in chapter 2, there seem to be more and more bulimics who are acknowledging their illness and are desperate in their overwhelming obsession. Therefore, a good deal of work is being initiated in group and individual therapies that combines behavioral and insight-oriented techniques. Self-help groups, usually with a recovered person as a leader or co-leader, seem to be helpful for some in coming to grips with the reality of the illness.

The strength of associations throughout the country lies in providing a network for professionals, sufferers, and families of sufferers, which in turn gives support and direction. Self-help groups are in themselves a symbol of taking responsibility for one's self and are a major step toward recovery. We look forward to a banding together of associations in the near future in some loose federation that may ensure a stable, continuing, and accessible source of help and support for families.

Cami Klein, a member of the American Anorexia/Bulimia Association, now co-leader in a self-help group, writes:

> The monthly self-help groups at the American Anorexia Bulimia Association (which I began attending in the beginning of 1979) eradicated the idea that my feelings and behavior were unique. What a shock to find myself in a room full of (mostly) women just like me! We all shared the same horrible secret, though the symptoms varied with each individual. I resisted the temptation to compete with the skinniest ones. Most amazing of all were the few who led the groups, because they had recovered. They weren't fat or ugly; in fact, they appeared more alive than most of the group members. They weren't happy all the time, but they dealt with their feelings directly, rather than suffocating themselves with too much food, or not enough. They weren't afraid of regressing anymore, because other things in life *really* were more important to them than how many calories they'd eaten, or what the scale said that day.

Now I am one of "them," and I, along with other recovered bulimics and anorexics, and professional therapists, lead the groups.

Cami has made the transition from a constricted life to a fuller, enriched way of living. Her identification is now with those who go on, dip into life, take risks, make mistakes, and enjoy. For the young women who see her and speak with her as she co-leads a self-help group, she has in turn become a model. Thus, we come full circle—and the process of maturity can go on. And in this process we truly can hear laughter again.

Appendix 1
Charts and Tables

1A. Percentage of Those Hospitalized, by Type of Eating Disorder

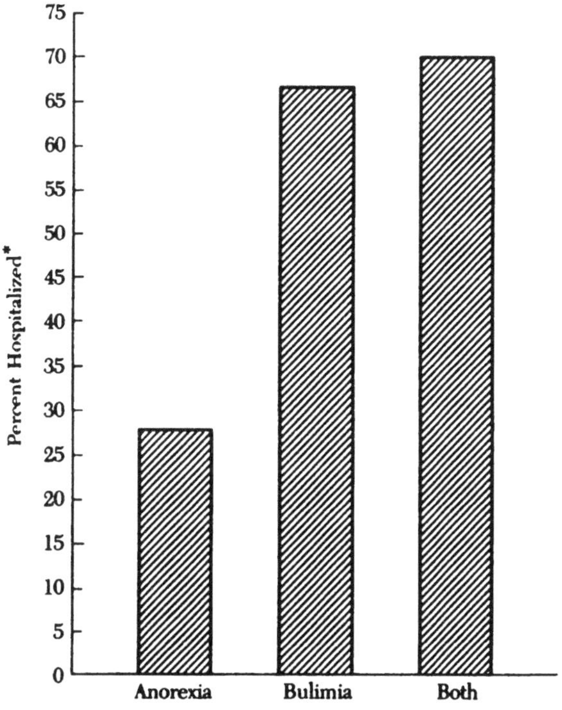

Source: Derived from responses to questionnaire sent by the American Anorexia/Bulimia Association to its Newsletter readers, 1981–82.

*Out of 158 families reporting, 92 percent reported their family member as having been hospitalized: 67 percent were reported as anorexic; 24 percent were reported as bulimic; and 69 percent were reported as both.

1B. Length of Hospitalization (First Admission), by Type of Eating Disorder

	Anorexia	Bulimia	Both	Total	Percentage*
Less than 30 days	18	2	6	26	28.3
30–59 days	12	1	10	23	25.0
60–89 days	3	0	3	6	6.5
90–119 days	7	1	4	12	13.0
120–149 days	3	0	3	6	6.5
150–179 days	5	0	2	7	7.5
180–359 days	5	0	3	8	8.7
360–720 days	0	1	1	2	2.2
Over 720 days	1	0	1	2	2.2
Total	54	5	33	92	100%

Source: Questionnaire.

*Out of 158 families answering this question, 58 percent reported hospitalization of the family member.

1C. Parents' Perceptions of the Helpfulness of Therapy for the 68 Percent of Children in Therapy

	Helpful		Somewhat Helpful		Not Helpful		Did Not Answer		Total	
	No.	%	No.	%	No.	%	No.	%	No.	%
Anorexia	47	74.6	8	12.7	4	6.3	4	6.3	63	100
Bulimia	10	47.6	5	23.8	3	14.3	3	14.3	21	100
Both	17	44.7	12	31.6	8	21.1	1	2.6	38	100
Total	74	60.7	25	20.5	15	12.3	8	6.6	122	100.1

Source: Questionnaire.

1D. Parent's with Weight Problems, as Reported by Parents

	No Weight Problem		Mom Only		Dad Only		Both Mom & Dad		Total	
	No.	%	No.	%	No.	%	No.	%	No.	%
Anorexia	44	54.3	27	33.3	6	7.4	4	4.9	81	99.9
Bulimia	13	56.5	8	34.8	2	8.7	0	0.0	23	100.0
Both	23	42.6	21	38.9	7	13	3	5.5	54	100
Total	80	50.6	56	35.4	15	9.5	7	4.4	158	99.9

Source: Questionnaire.

1E. Parents with Weight Problems, Alcohol Problems, Both, or Neither, as Reported by Parents

	Weight Problem		Alcohol Problem		Both		Neither		Total
	No.	%	No.	%	No.	%	No.	%	Number
Anorexia	37	45.7	19	23.5	9	11.1	34	42	81
Bulimia	10	43.5	3	13	3	13	13	56.5	23
Both	31	57.4	13	24.1	9	16.7	19	35.2	54
Total	78	49.4	35	22.2	21	13.3	66	41.8	158

Source: Questionnaire.

1F. Income Level Reported by 162 Families

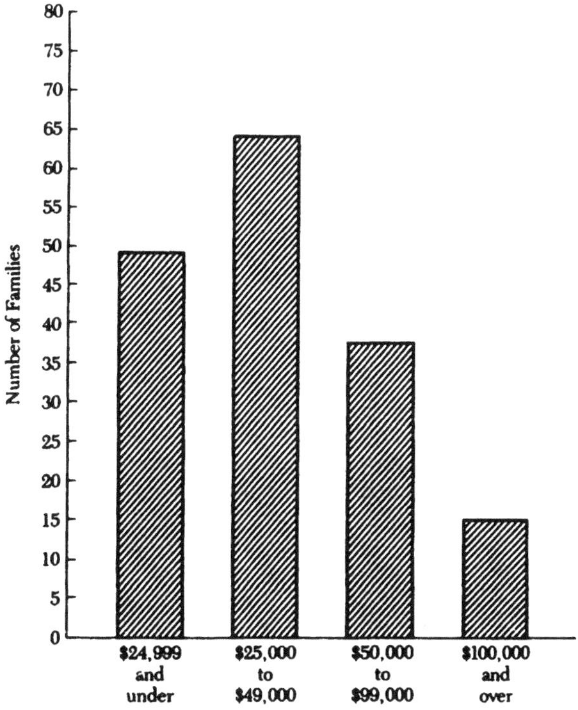

Source: Questionnaire.

Appendix 2: Addresses

HEADQUARTERS
American Anorexia/Bulimia Association, Inc.
133 Cedar Lane
Teaneck, NJ 07666
(201) 836-1800

AFFILIATES
Florida
Lisaann Shapiro-Dorfman
9220 Andora Drive
Miramar, FL 33025
(305) 431-3889

Georgia
American Anorexia Nervosa Association of Atlanta
Ann Bradshaw, M.Div., President
3533 Kingsboro Road, N.E.
Atlanta, GA 30319
(404) 266-8779

Massachusetts
Barbara Remmers
472 Memorial Drive, Room 212
Cambridge, MA 02139

New York
A.A.B.A. Self-Help Group

Lori Levy, M.S.W.
Lenox Hill Hospital
172 E. 91st Street
New York, NY 10028
(212) 289-0027

Donna Pauldine
Rockland Community Mental Health Center
Pomona, NY 10970
(914) 354-0200, ext. 2240

Pennsylvania

American Anorexia Bulimia Association of Philadelphia, Inc.
Elizabeth Chace, Coordinator
Philadelphia Child Guidance Clinic
34th & Civic Center Boulevard
Philadelphia, PA 19104
(215) 387-1919

Joan Bizousky, RN, MA.
1000 Woodland
Punxsutawney, PA 15767

Virginia

Carolyn Franck
Martinsville & Henry County Mental Health Association
117 Broad Street
Martinsville, VA 24112

AABA of Tidewater, VA
Riverside Hospital CMHC
Mary Ann Sipe, Coordinator
420 J. Clyde Morris Boulevard
Newport News, VA 23601
(804) 595-4435

For further information about resources call or write the association's main office or an affiliate near you. Your local medical and mental health center or mental health association may also have information.

References

Atwood, Margaret. 1969. *The Edible Woman*. Toronto: Seal Books and Steward-Bantam. (Fiction)

Bruch, Hilde. 1973. *Eating Disorders: Obesity, Anorexia Nervosa, and the Person Within*. New York: Basic Books.

——1978. *The Golden Cage*. Cambridge: Harvard University Press.

Crisp, Arthur H. 1980. *Anorexia Nervosa: Let Me Be*. London, Toronto, and Sydney: Academic Press; New York and San Francisco: Grune and Stratton.

de Beauvoir, Simone. 1972. *The Coming of Age*. Patrick O'Brien, tr. New York: Putnam.

Erikson, Erik H. 1963. *Childhood and Society*. New York: Norton.

Ewen, Stuart and Elizabeth Ewen. 1982. *Channels of Desire*. New York: McGraw-Hill.

Garfinkel, Paul E. and David M. Garner. 1982. *Anorexia Nervosa: A Multidimensional Perspective*. New York: Brunner/Mazel.

Hammer, Signe. 1982. *Passionate Attachments: Fathers and Daughters in America Today*. New York: Rawson.

Huebner, Hans. 1981. Speech for the American Anorexia Nervosa Association.

MacLeod, Sheila. 1982. *The Art of Starvation: A Story of Anorexia and Survival*. London and New York: Schocken.

Mahler, Margaret S. 1968. In collaboration with Manuel Furer, M.D. *On Human Symbiosis and the Vicissitudes of Individuation*. Vol. 1, *Infantile Psychosis*. New York: International Universities Press.

Mahler, Margaret S., Fred Pine, and Anni Bergman. 1975. *Psychological Birth of the Human Infant*. New York: Basic Books.

Millman, Marcia. 1980. *Such a Pretty Face*. New York: Norton.

Orbach, Suzie. 1978. *Fat Is a Feminist Issue*. New York: Paddington Press, Berkeley Medallion Books.

Palazzoli, Mara Selvini. 1978. *Self Starvation: From Individual to Family Therapy in the Treatment of Anorexia Nervosa*. Arnold Pomerans, tr. New York: Jason Aronson; London: Human Context Books, Chaucer Publishing, 1974.

Schwartz, Donald, Michael J. Thompson, and Craig L. Johnson. 1982. "Anorexia Nervosa and Bulimia: The Socio-Cultural Context." *International Journal of Eating Disorders* (Spring) 1(3):20–35.

Sours, John A. 1980. *Starving to Death in a Sea of Objects: The Anorexia Nervosa Syndrome*. New York and London: Jason Aronson. (First part fiction, remainder a description of anorexia nervosa syndrome.)

Wilson, Charles Philip. 1982. "The Fear of Being Fat and Anorexia Nervosa," *International Journal of Psychoanalytic Psychotherapy*, 9:233–255.

Wurtman, Judith J., Richard J. Wurtman, John H. Growdon, Peter Henry, Anne Lipscomb, and Steven H. Zeisel. 1981. "Carbohydrate Craving in Obese People: Suppression by Treatments Affecting Serotoninergic Transmission." *International Journal of Eating Disorders* (Autumn), 1(1):2–12.

Suggested Reading

Current literature about anorexia nervosa and bulimia: professional and nonprofessional, fictional and nonfictional, and autobiographical writings. We have added some which discuss weight and weight consciousness for background to the many issues that eating disorders raise in our present society.

Nonfiction

Boskind-White, Marlene and William C. White, Jr. *Bulimarexia: The Binge/Purge Cycle*. New York and London: Norton, 1983.

Bruch, Hilde. *Eating Disorders: Obesity, Anorexia Nervosa, and the Person Within*. New York: Basic Books, 1973.

——*The Golden Cage: The Enigma of Anorexia Nervosa*. Cambridge: Harvard University Press, 1978.

Cauwels, Janice M. *Bulimia: The Binge Purge Compulsion*. Garden City, N.Y.: Doubleday, 1983.

Chernin, Kim. *The Obsession: Reflections on the Tyranny of Slenderness*. New York: Harper and Row, 1981.

Crisp, Arthur H. *Anorexia Nervosa: Let Me Be*. London, Toronto, and Sydney: Academic Press; New York and San Francisco: Grune and Stratton, 1980.

Dally, Peter and Joan Gomez. *Obesity and Anorexia Nervosa: A Question of Shape*. London and Boston: Faber & Faber, 1980.

Garfinkel, Paul E. and David M. Garner. *Anorexia Nervosa: A Multidimensional Perspective*. New York: Brunner/Mazel, 1982.

Gross, Meier, ed. *Anorexia Nervosa*. Lexington, Mass: D. C. Heath, Collamore Press, 1982.

International Journal of Eating Disorders. Craig Johnson, ed. New York: Van Nostrand, 1981. A quarterly publication.

Landau, Elaine. *Why Are They Starving Themselves?* New York: Messner, 1983.

Langs, Robert, ed., *International Journal of Psychoanalytic Psychotherapy*, vol.

9: C. Philip Wilson, "The Fear of Being Fat and Anorexia Nervosa," pp. 233–255; Cecil Mushatt, "Anorexia Nervosa: A Psychoanalytic Commentary," pp. 258–265; Ian Story, "Anorexia Nervosa and the Psychotherapeutic Hospital," 268–302; Hilde Bruch, "Treatment in Anorexia Nervosa," pp. 303–312.

Levenkron, Steven. *Treating and Overcoming Anorexia Nervosa*. New York: Scribner, 1982; Warner, 1983.

Minuchin, Salvador, Bernice L. Rosman, and Lester Baker. *Psychosomatic Families: Anorexia Nervosa in Context*. Cambridge: Harvard University Press, 1978.

Neuman, Patricia A. and Patricia A. Halvorson. *Anorexia Nervosa and Bulimia: A Handbook for Counselors and Therapists*. New York: Van Nostrand Rheinhold, 1983.

Palazzoli, Mara Selvini. *Self-Starvation: From Individual to Family Therapy in the Treatment of Anorexia Nervosa*. Arnold Pomerans, tr. New York and London: Jason Aronson, 1978; London: Human Context Books, Chaucer, 1974.

Palmer, R. E. *Anorexia Nervosa*. New York: Penguin, 1980.

Roth, Geneen. *Feeding the Hungry Heart: The Experience of Compulsive Eating*. Indianapolis/New York: Bobbs-Merrill, 1982.

Sours, John A. *Starving to Death in a Sea of Objects: The Anorexia Nervosa Syndrome*. New York and London: Jason Aronson, 1980.

Sperling, Melitta. *Psychosomatic Disorders in Childhood*. New York and London: Jason Aronson, 1978.

Squire, Susan. *The Slender Balance*. New York: Putnam, 1983.

Thomä, Helmut. *Anorexia Nervosa*. New York: International Universities Press, 1967.

Vigersky, Robert. *Anorexia Nervosa*. New York: Raven Press, 1977.

Wilson, Charles Philip with the assistance of Charles C. Hogan, and Ira L. Mintz. *The Fear of Being Fat: The Treatment of Anorexia and Bulimia*. New York: Jason Aronson, 1983.

Fiction

Hautzig, Deborah. *Second Star to the Right*. New York: Greenwillow Books, 1981.

Josephs, Rebecca. *Early Disorder*. New York: Farrar Straus and Giroux, 1980.

Levenkron, Steven. *The Best Little Girl in the World*. Chicago: Contemporary Books, 1978.

Autobiography

Latimer, Jane Evans. *Reflections on Recovery: Freedom from Bulimia and Compulsive Overeating*. Dallas, Texas: Mesa Productions, 1983.

Liu, Aimee. *Solitaire*. New York: Harper and Row, 1979.

MacLeod, Sheila. *The Art of Starvation: A Story of Anorexia and Survival*. New York: Schocken Books, 1982.

Heater, Sandra H. *Am I Still Visible?* While Hall, Va.: Betterway, 1983.

O'Neill, Cherry Boone. *Starving for Attention.* New York: Continuum Books, 1982.

Rumney, Auis. *Dying to Please: Anorexia Nervosa and Its Cure.* Jefferson, N.C.: McFarland, 1983.

Related Subjects

Bennett, William G. and Joel Gurin. *Dieter's Dilemma: Eating Less and Weighing More.* New York: Basic Books, 1982.

Millman, Marcia. *Such a Pretty Face: Being Fat in America.* New York and London: Norton, 1980.

Orbach, Suzie. *Fat Is a Feminist Issue.* New York: Paddington Press; Berkeley Medallion Books, 1978.

Powers, Pauline S. *Obesity: The Regulation of Weight.* Baltimore and London: Williams and Wilkins, 1980.

Zales, Michael R., ed. *Eating, Sleeping, and Sexuality.* New York: Brunner/Mazel, 1982.

Index

Bei Fragen zur Produktsicherheit wenden Sie sich bitte an:
If you have any questions regarding product safety,
please contact:

Walter de Gruyter GmbH
Genthiner Straße 13
10785 Berlin
productsafety@degruyterbrill.com